Mindful Muslim

Embrace Daily Habits to Nurture
Your Soul for a Balanced Life
Filled with Joy & Gratitude

SARAH GULFRAZ

Copyright © 2024 Sarah Gulfraz

Sarah Gulfraz has asserted her right to be identified as the author of this Work in accordance with the Copyright, Designs and Patents Act 1988.

All rights reserved.

No portion of this book may be reproduced in any form, stored in a retrieval system, stored in a database, or published/transmitted in any form or by any means, electronic, mechanical, photocopying, recording or otherwise, without prior written permission of the publisher.

Contents

Dedication	IV
1. Introduction	1
2. Mindfulness in Islam	4
3. Morning Rituals for Spiritual Awakening	23
4. Daily Quranic Reflections	38
5. Dhikr & Remembrance of Allah (SWT)	50
6. Mindful Eating and Nutrition	60
7. Self-Care and Well-Being	72
8. Mindfulness in Prayer and Salah	85
9. Practising Patience and Gratitude	93
10. Mindful Communication and Relationships	106
11. Evening Reflection and Gratitude Practice	117
12. Conclusion	129
Find Out More	132

Dedication

~ **Bismillah** ~

May Allah (swt) accept our efforts and grant us success in this life and the next. Ameen.

In dedication to my loving family and all their support.

Chapter One

Introduction

Modern life is full of constant noise, distraction, and resource overload. For some of us, even a brief period of peaceful silence seems unattainable due to the constant stimulation of our senses.

This constant agitation reduces the quality of our prayers and our capacity to remember Allah (SWT), preventing us from making the most of every minute.

But we should remember that the purpose of the dunya is to divert our attention. Every day is an examination by Allah (SWT) to separate the good from the evil. Someone may claim that they are too preoccupied with making a life to keep Allah (SWT) in mind.

We must, of course, go to work. But there is a significant distinction between working and being linked to Allah (SWT) and being so consumed by one's work that one forgets about Him.

When we labour, we should not cut off our ties to Allah (SWT). Work and Allah (SWT) are not two separate entities; we can do both. Allah calls on believers to always remember Him in the Quran:

> "So remember me, and I will remember you. And thank me, and do not be ungrateful." (Quran 2:152)

The Quran was revealed through the Prophet (PBUH), and according to Hazrat Aisha (RA), he would constantly remember Allah (SWT) no matter what he was doing. His attention was focused on constantly remembering Him.

> *Aisha (RA) reported that the Prophet (PBUH) would remember Allah at all times. (Sahih Muslim)*

We all acknowledge that we need to be more present in prayer and exert greater control over our straying thoughts and impulses. However, how precisely can we accomplish this? How can we practise mindfulness in our spiritual and worldly lives?

This is where the potency of the mutually beneficial interaction between Islamic spirituality and mindfulness lies; it is a potent tool for mental health. By combining Islamic teachings with the practice of self-reflection and presence, one can achieve more resilience, emotional control, and inner serenity.

This healthy relationship encourages everyone to pursue the path to a deeper and more fulfilling life and investigate Islam's teachings and ideals. Islam is more than just a religion; it is a wellspring of enduring knowledge, awareness, and spiritual harmony.

In Islam, the basis of the interaction between believers and Allah (SWT) is thought to be attentiveness. It is an essential idea in Islam and aids in developing piety among followers of the faith. Being fully present in the moment and becoming more conscious of one's thoughts, feelings, and behaviours are two aspects of mindfulness.

The goal is to have a close relationship with Allah (SWT). Muslims need to practise mindfulness and attention to improve their relationship with Allah (SWT) in the fast-paced, frantic world of today.

MINDFUL MUSLIM

In Islam, mindfulness is not a new concept but rather a significant essence of Islamic teachings. Despite being a buzzword in today's world, people are still unaware of the significance of this idea in Islam, ways to incorporate it into their lives, and its impact on life. In this book, we will explore mindfulness rooted in Islamic teaching, aiming to foster a more balanced, fulfilling life.

This book seeks to lead you through everyday routines based on Islamic teachings on mindfulness and spiritual development. In accordance with Islamic teachings, each chapter examines doable tactics, rituals, and introspective exercises to nourish your soul (Nafs) and heighten your spiritual awareness.

Through the incorporation of mindfulness practices into your everyday routine, you can improve your relationship with Allah (SWT) and feel a deeper sense of peace, thankfulness, and purpose in life. These pages are intended to support you in deepening your faith and reflecting on your spiritual journey, regardless of how experienced you are as a Muslim or where you are in your spiritual journey.

This book covers a wide range of themes, such as forgiveness and gratitude, mindfulness and self-improvement, and spiritual practice, with Hadiths, verses from the Quran, and more. Use this resource to begin your spiritual journey. Learn how daily introspection, prayer, and action may alter. It contains everything you need to become more conscious and strengthen your faith.

Let's dive in!

Chapter Two

Mindfulness in Islam

Understanding Mindfulness in the Islamic Context

In today's hyperconnected society, our thoughts and the pleasures of life constantly divert us. It is uncommon for someone to always be fully present in the moment. Furthermore, the social media devices we own add to our inability to concentrate on the here and now.

In actuality, we lose 41% of our waking hours to our thoughts, which are primarily focused on the past and future rather than the here and now. Due to this constant barrage of information or distraction, we cannot be productive and maximise every moment.

As humans, we have the propensity to be highly self-centred. We easily become so engrossed in our issues and egos that we forget who Allah (SWT) is. We stop focusing on Allah (SWT) when we focus too much on ourselves.

This hectic world offers us countless opportunities to stray from our faith. We drift away from Allah (SWT) when we stop being focused on our faith. Muslims must consider faith as a motivation. Who wants to ride with a driver that is distracted? Numerous things are possible. You fail to make your exits. You go off the path. You make a mistaken turn. As a Muslim, our faith is the same. Spiritual diversion can take many different forms and lead us down many different pathways that lead us away from Allah (SWT).

So, every Muslim must ask themselves: How can I focus and exert more control over my straying thoughts? How can I live more intentionally in both my spiritual and temporal spheres?

This is where practising mindfulness, also known as Muraqabah in the Islamic context, can help us educate our thoughts to become more disciplined, increasing our productivity in all our activities, including daily devotion.

Islam provides people with divine guidance for harmonious living in this world and the next, addressing both their spiritual and material needs. Islamic teachings provide the groundwork for constructive interpersonal relationships and a well-adjusted societal structure. They are an ideal system that perfectly suits human nature.

By heeding these lessons, we can enhance our own and other people's lives. The practice of mindfulness is one such lesson. While mindfulness is necessary in all aspects of life, some situations require it more than others.

Definition of mindfulness in Islam and its spiritual significance

Linguistically, mindfulness is the state or quality of being conscious or aware of something; more precisely, mindfulness is a mental state attained as a therapeutic technique by focusing one's awareness on the present moment while quietly acknowledging and embracing one's feelings, ideas, and bodily sensations.

From an Islamic perspective, mindfulness is primarily about spiritual well-being. We believe it may support our mental and emotional health and is firmly anchored in our awareness of and relationship with Allah (SWT).

Simply put, mindfulness is the capacity to focus on the here and now without becoming sidetracked by all the visible feelings, ideas, and emotions. While this practice can significantly benefit our emotional well-being, for us as Muslims, its mainstream interpretation of mindfulness is insufficient in the absence of Allah (SWT).

Through attentive observation of our thoughts and emotions, we can learn to modify our mental models, or cognitive processes, to our advantage. When we are not paying attention, we respond to ideas and feelings automatically and allow them to take us in any direction they want. On the other hand, developing a state of mindfulness will enable us to choose whether or not to follow our thoughts.

Even in a neutral or nonreligious setting, practising mindfulness has been shown to have quantifiable positive effects on one's health and well-being. Within the Islamic faith, mindfulness is associated with the virtue of Muraqabah, a word whose fundamental meaning is to watch, observe, and scrutinise intently.

The goal of Muraqabah is to become more conscious of every thought, action, and statement we make. It identifies our cognitive styles, susceptibility to influences, and emotional states and assesses the degree of excellence in each of these areas.

Its role is to stand at the threshold of our consciousness, protecting it from anything that could cause us to lose sight of Allah (SWT) and allowing the currents to carry us nearer to our creator.

Knowing that Allah (SWT) is constantly keeping an eye on us leads to a higher awareness and concern for our behaviours, thoughts, feelings, and interior states of being, which is the foundation of Muraqabah. It focuses on establishing a connection between our body, mind, and soul to enhance our emotional and spiritual well-being.

As Allah says in the Quran: *"And know that Allah knows what is within yourselves, so beware of Him. And know that Allah is Forgiving and Forbearing."* (Quran 2:235)

In another place, Allah (SWT) says about mindfulness in the Quran:

"And you are not engaged in any matter or recite any of the Quran, and you do not do any deed except that we are witness over you when you are involved in it. And not absent from your Lord is any part of an atom's weight within the earth or within the heaven or anything smaller than that or greater but that it is in a clear register." (Quran 10:61)

In this sense, mindfulness means being continuously conscious of Allah's (SWT) omnipresence and His observation of everything we do. This awareness encourages a person to act righteously and sincerely, knowing that Allah (SWT) is aware of even the smallest details of their actions and intentions.

Furthermore, mindfulness is a mental state in which you refine and accept your thoughts by concentrating on the here and now. Contrary to what the name might imply, the goal is to separate your thoughts and focus on each one individually. Islam understands mindfulness in terms of its four facets.

- Understanding Allah (SWT)
- Understanding your soul
- Understanding evil (Shayṭan)
- Understanding what good activities one should perform for Allah's (SWT) sake

In essence, it is the capacity to focus on the here and now without becoming sidetracked by all the thoughts, feelings, distractions, and emotions we encounter. From the standpoint of emotional health, Muslims can benefit greatly from this idea. But for us Muslims, this conventional interpretation of mindfulness is devoid of Allah (SWT).

The Quran asks us to practise mindfulness both in our daily lives and throughout our extended human journey. Islam is the source of higher awareness, expanded thinking, and progressive viewpoint expansion. The Quran serves as a reminder that Allah (SWT) is All-Seeing and All-Knowing.

> *"Indeed, Allah knows the unseen [aspects] of the heavens and the earth. And Allah is Seeing of what you do."*
> *(Quran 49:18)*

Through the Quran, we are given clues to broaden our thinking and increase our awareness of the Majesty of our Creator and His absolute control over all aspects of reality. Coincidences result from human error that is not purposeful.

Using the Quran as a guide, we understand that Allah (SWT) is the Most Intentional and that the idea of coincidence is unworthy of His Almighty Wisdom and Power.

This supports the idea that every indication we receive, every time we are instructed to exercise caution, and every time we are told to trust in something more than what is immediately apparent or obvious—all of these things are extremely important because Allah (SWT) has specifically chosen these details to support our beliefs and strengthen our Iman (Faith).

> *Narrated by Abdullah Ibn Abbas (RA): "One day, I was behind the Prophet (PBUH), and he said: Be mindful of*

Allah, and He will take care of you. Be mindful of Allah, and you shall find Him with you." (Tirmidhi)

It supports the idea that every event and every caution given to us is significant and intentional, chosen by Allah (SWT) to strengthen our faith and understanding.

Allah (SWT) encourages observation, contemplation, and a broader view. However, some individuals may be more inclined to follow their own desires (the human ego) rather than the signs of Allah (SWT). If this behaviour is not stopped, one eventually gets engrossed in gratifying their needs or engaged in themselves.

This is a further diversion from surrendering to Allah's (SWT) will. Rather than using mindfulness to remain in a state of Allah's (SWT) consciousness and attain happiness in both this life and the afterlife, time, effort, and energy should be dedicated to connecting with the Divine.

Not every idea or emotion we experience is constructive or calls for action. Humans are susceptible to whispers from angels who wish us good and from Shayṭan and his army, which might influence us. In light of this, we must be acutely conscious of our emotions and thoughts. We must be aware of what thoughts are entering our minds and consciously reject the unfavourable ones that may lead us astray.

The concept of mindfulness is not merely theoretical; it also necessitates decisive action, both externally and mostly inside. Modern mindfulness and Islamic mindfulness are very different from one another.

While Islamic mindfulness promotes an increase in consciousness of Allah (SWT) for Allah's (SWT) sake, modern mindfulness fosters self-validation for reasons of self. At the same time, the latter will benefit people both in this world and the next, and the former will benefit people in this life.

Mindfulness and Spirituality

Pursuing inner peace and a sense of direction have become more crucial in our hectic, often chaotic world. Many resort to spirituality and mindfulness activities to cultivate a stronger sense of self-connection and awareness of their surroundings.

Mindfulness can be seen as a tool that strengthens and supports spiritual experiences, while spirituality offers a framework for comprehending and applying mindfulness in daily life. Spirituality and mindfulness are intimately related.

Spiritualism and mindfulness both provide transforming paths to inner serenity and a more fulfilled life because of their emphasis on current consciousness and connection to something greater than themselves.

While mindfulness practice enhances spiritual experiences and advancement, spirituality enriches them. Let's take a look at the relationship between spirituality and mindfulness, focusing on how they work together to promote inner peace and presence.

Spirituality and mindfulness complement and enhance one another's advantages in a mutually beneficial way. Being completely conscious of one's thoughts, feelings, physical sensations, and the surroundings around oneself is referred to as mindfulness. Conversely, spirituality is a more comprehensive notion that includes pursuing meaning, purpose, and a connection to something more than oneself.

It can be articulated through religious convictions, but it also encompasses personal thoughts and activities beyond organised religion. Investigating issues related to the nature of existence, the purpose of life, and the development of inner serenity are common components of spirituality.

The practice of mindfulness fosters present-moment awareness, which is essential for strengthening spiritual ties and enhancing spiritual experiences. It aids in the development of the ability to notice and release distractions, making people more open to spiritual revelations and experiences. Spirituality improves mindfulness practice by providing a more expansive context and intentionality of growing awareness.

It provides a framework for people to investigate existential issues, incorporate mindfulness into their daily lives, and give their practice a sense of direction and significance. When combined, spirituality and mindfulness have a positive effect on one's general health and increase one's awareness of the world and oneself. Accept incorporating spirituality and mindfulness into your everyday life to start this life-changing path of self-discovery, connection, and deep calm.

From an Islamic perspective, it is more crucial to prioritise spiritual well-being above mental and emotional health since it is believed to most effectively support our emotional health and is firmly anchored in our knowledge of and connection to Allah (SWT).

Remember that mindfulness goes beyond focusing on the brain and its role in habit formation and overall well-being. Islam holds that our hearts are the source of our awareness of Allah (SWT).

> *Once, the Holy Prophet (PBUH) pointed to his heart and said: "Mindfulness of Allah is here, and he pointed to his chest three times." (Sahih Muslim)*

Furthermore, since it calls for concentration and awareness, setting an intention is a mindfulness practice. Muslims are taught that the motives behind an action determine its outcome.

According to the teachings of our Prophet (PBUH), whatever we do is done for Allah's (SWT) pleasure and has to be good for us or other people. Making intentions on a spiritual level gives us the energy, inspiration, and drive to perform to the best of our abilities.

> As Ibn Attaullah said: *"Actions are lifeless forms, but the presence of an inner sincerity is what endows us with life-giving spirit." (Kitab Al Hikam)*

And what motivates us to make amends and present our best selves to serve Allah (SWT) and His creation—at work or home—is the awareness of our final home and the Day of Judgement.

> *Abdullah ibn Umair (RA) narrates that the Messenger of Allah (PBUH) said: "Whoever makes an intention for the sake of the world; Allah, the Exalted, brings poverty before him and leaves it desiring it. Whoever makes the afterlife his intention; Allah, the exalted, makes his heart rich and gathers him with what he lost then he leaves with more abstinence from it." (Ibn Majah)*

This emphasises that the true value and spirit of actions lie in their intentions. It underscores that sincerity and the purpose behind our actions endow them with true spiritual significance.

Nurturing the soul (nafs) through mindful practices

The Arabic word "nafs" (which means "self") is a notion that is central to Islamic spirituality and theology. Islam places great emphasis on the idea of nafs, which describes an individual's inner nature.

It is an intricate idea that encompasses a range of human experiences, including moral, spiritual, and psychological ones. It is believed that nafs are fundamental to human identity and personality and that they are a necessary step on the path to spiritual fulfilment.

It is a blend of good and terrible under one's control. Depending on the specifics of the conflict between the evil and lordly souls occurring in his inner dimension, a man directs his life. When the lordly soul triumphs, man tends toward morality and good acts. But when the evil soul takes control, man gets attracted towards all forms of evil and immorality.

Man is accountable for his deeds because of his choices and inclinations between right and wrong; man is responsible for his actions and subject to both reward and punishment because he has the ability to use free will to carry out his activities and, in doing so, govern his evil soul to some degree.

Allah tells us this: By the Nafs (Soul), and the proportion and order given to it; and its enlightenment to understand what is right and wrong for it. (Quran 91:7-8)

Without a doubt, Allah (SWT) gave us traits and attributes that make us unique from other creations. The human being, for instance, was endowed with a qalb, or heart, which was made only for the purpose of knowing and loving Allah (SWT), and an 'Aql, or mind, which allowed him to be capable of knowledge and comprehension.

The capacity to discern between good and wrong—the capacity to make decisions—was also innate in the human race. Most of Allah's (SWT) other creations did not have this choice. Without the ability to act otherwise, everything—including rocks, plants, animals, rain, wind, water, and even angels—submits to Allah's (SWT) commands and will. The existence of the nafs gives us the capacity to distinguish between right and wrong.

Fortunately, our nafs is conscious. We are in charge of the choices we make that affect both this life and the next. As a result, always keep Allah (SWT) in mind and choose to resist your undesirable impulses and wants.

This concept is referenced in Surah Al-Rome, where it is highlighted that the inherent nature of humans cannot be altered. Islam's nature is inherent in every human being, and this nature never changes. The real change is in the nafs, which can become tainted when one strays from the right path. We must clean our nafs to restore its purity, as it can become tainted repeatedly. This issue is not human nature but the condition of the nafs. All people, regardless of race, ethnicity, or country of origin, are inherently good because they are created by Allah (SWT).

Occasionally, the nafs present us with a choice: either we take charge of our nafs, or the nafs take control of us. Either our nafs rule us, or we rule our nafs. The nafs overwhelms us when it becomes contaminated, and we fail to purge it of contaminants.

However, as long as we remain vigilant, and keep an eye on things—let us take an example—any aspirations or wishes you may have will be assessed and reviewed by the individual in question. Is this a nice wish, and is it the correct wish? Is it beneficial or detrimental? If it is a good wish, then praise be to Allah; if not, I must get rid of that desire and cleanse myself.

Thus, "Tazkiyahh" (cleansing the nafs) involves getting rid of your negative desires. The act of purifying oneself, or Tazkiyahh, is the removal of impurities. Tazkiyahh, also known as purification, is the process of ridding oneself of any impurities of the heart, such as incorrect desires, evil intentions, or a need to flaunt oneself. We refer to it as repentance. People consider how to enhance themselves and develop into better people. This is the entire procedure, and it must to be followed.

> *And the soul and Him Who perfected it; and that inspired her licentiousness and piety! In truth, the man who purifies his soul will be saved. (Quran 91: 7–9)*

In Islam, developing a holy character largely depends on one's ability to exercise self-control and accountability. It is crucial for Muslims to understand how to combat desire (nafs) in Islam. It includes numerous additional elements as well as religious customs. To live in accordance with Allah's will, we must adhere to the teachings of Islam.

Without question, leading a controlled life enables us to succeed both here on Earth and in the afterlife. We must gain a thorough understanding of Jihad Bin Nafs. Muslims must constantly cleanse themselves to maintain their attention on the path of righteousness.

It is said that when we are mindful and fully present in the moment, we have a deeper comprehension of what is happening and start to feel acceptance, joy, peace, and love. Managing work and daily life can be too much at times. The responsibilities of modern life, including work, relationships, and family, can deplete our vitality.

It is simple to disregard caring for our body, mind, and spirit. Nonetheless, preserving a state of equilibrium among these three components is essential to attaining holistic prosperity and elevating our spiritual force. Investigating the value of fostering these facets of who we are and looking at doable strategies are crucial.

Nurturing the nafs through mindfulness can transform your soul. Practise meditation daily, focusing on your breath to calm the mind. Keep a gratitude journal to shift your focus to positivity. Engage in mindful breathing and body scans to ground yourself and release tension.

Mindful walking in nature enhances presence, while loving-kindness meditation fosters compassion. Reflect on spiritual texts and practise mindful eating to appreciate nourishment. Spend time in silence and solitude for inner peace and engage in creative expression to explore emotions. These practices cultivate inner peace, spiritual growth, and a deeper connection with yourself and the world.

Benefits of Mindfulness for Muslims

The advantages of mindfulness are well-publicised, and you will hear many people discuss how it improves their mental, emotional, and spiritual well-being. You learn via mindfulness that your ideas and feelings are not the same as who you are. You are the one who is observing your emotions and ideas. You get better at putting your thoughts and feelings aside. This mental distance makes it possible for you to react to life intelligently rather than rashly. To assist you in understanding the significance of mindfulness in Islam, let's look at these benefits.

Enhancing spiritual awareness and connection with Allah (Taqarrub)

It takes intentional measures to develop our faith and establish a deep connection with Allah (SWT). Frequent prayer and Quran recitation serve as a reminder of our life's purpose as well as the ideals and standards we ought to pursue. We can speak with Allah (SWT) through these acts of worship and ask for His blessings and guidance.

As Muslims, we recognise the significance of maintaining a close relationship with Allah (SWT). Building a relationship with our Creator can significantly influence our lives, not merely following rituals. One of the most exquisite Islamic rituals is the dua. We, as Muslims, can use dua to communicate with our Creator.

It is the most effective means of supplicating, communicating, and calling upon Allah (SWT). For believers, the dua is an essential component of Islam since it not only builds a bridge between the servants and the Lord but also between an individual and themselves.

The Prophet Muhammad (PBUH) said: "The most excellent worship is Dua." (Sahih Al-Jami)

Allah (SWT) is not inaccessible; instead, He is very near to us; all we need to do is perform good deeds that may point us in His direction.

Allah (SWT) says in the Quran: "And when my servants ask you, concerning me - indeed I am near. I respond to the invocation of the supplicant when he calls upon me. So let them respond to me (by obedience) and believe in me that they may be [rightly] guided". (Quran 2:186)

Allah (SWT) has repeatedly stated in the Quran that He is with us wherever we go and that we should call on Him at any time, no matter what. Muslims only need to remember their Creator and do as they are told to stay in constant communication with Him.

Even Muslims can perform dua whenever they like; it is not required to do so after Iftar following a fast or after Salah. Islam is the simplest religion because it offers far too easy ways to have a closer relationship with Allah (SWT).

You can use your Islamic knowledge to strengthen your spiritual connection with Allah (SWT) during salah (prayer). By practising mindful breathing and concentration techniques, concentrate on strengthening your relationship. Keep a rigid schedule and give your full attention to the act of worship. Find out more about Allah's (SWT) qualities to deepen your spiritual connection.

To truly experience the thrill of worshipping Allah (SWT), give your prayers a purpose and cultivate a sense of respect. Accept His love and compassion to attain inner peace and joy. By being observant during salah, you can enhance your prayer experience and strengthen your relationship with Him. On this road of spiritual development, there are yet more revelations to come.

We can also fortify our relationship with Allah (SWT) by performing deeds of love and generosity. Not only does helping the less fortunate benefit them, but it also purifies our spirits, strengthens our faith, and increases our humility.

Above all, a genuine commitment to our religion and loyalty to Allah (SWT) is necessary for maintaining a connection with Him. It entails admitting our own frailties and limits and pleading for Allah's (SWT) pardon and mercy. It also entails making a deliberate effort to better ourselves and the people around us and trying to live our lives in accordance with Islamic principles.

In sum, developing a relationship with Allah (SWT) is a personal path that necessitates us taking charge of maintaining our religion. We may lead meaningful lives, inspire and mentor people around us, and realise our own desires by dedicating our lives to Allah (SWT) and His teachings.

By means of these practices, Muslims can quiet the mind, become more spiritually aware, and establish a deeper connection with the divine presence. In addition to enhancing the prayer experience, this elevated state of mindfulness fosters inner serenity and a feeling of intimacy with Allah (SWT).

Deepening Connection with Allah (SWT)

It takes a deep comprehension of Allah's (SWT) qualities as well as a genuine desire to fortify your spiritual bond via prayer and reflection to deepen your relationship with Him. You can have closer contact with the Divine by exploring the depths of His attributes, such as Ar-Rahman (The Most Merciful) as well as Al-Ghaffar (The Forgiving). Connecting more deeply is a journey towards inner calm and spiritual development rather than just a laborious exercise.

When you try to comprehend Allah's (SWT) unending love and compassion, you become receptive to His unlimited mercy and forgiveness. This understanding can help you feel at ease and satisfied in your spirit, promoting inner serenity that surpasses material worries.

Prayer, introspection, and mindfulness can help you develop a strong relationship with Allah (SWT) and navigate the ups and downs of life. In essence, developing your connection with Allah (SWT) is a transforming process that enhances your spiritual journey, develops your soul, and leads you to enlightenment and contentment.

Improving mental clarity, focus, and emotional well-being

Maintaining mental resilience is more important than ever in a time of uncertainty, stress, and misfortune. Islam provides priceless ideas and customs that support this enduring power. Together with resilience, taqwa—a type of mindfulness—forms a potent combination that strengthens mental health and resilience. By exploring this fascinating relationship, we extend a warm invitation to comprehend and accept the profound wisdom of Islam.

Islam's core idea of taqwa, which is frequently translated as "piety" or "Allah-consciousness," highlights a person's awareness of Allah (SWT) in all facets of life and promotes deeds and ideas consistent with virtue and faith. Resilience is the ability to adjust, bounce back, and prosper in the face of hardship. It makes it possible for individuals to triumph gracefully and resolutely over obstacles in life.

Resilience, combined with taqwa, provides a potent source of unbreakable mental strength. By combining faith-based values with the ability to adjust, conquer, and endure, a person can face obstacles in life with grace and tenacity. This incredible link is an invitation to study Islamic teachings and principles and a route to increased psychological fortitude.

Being mindful makes you more conscious of your thoughts and emotions. Being self-aware enables you to act with greater sincerity because it helps you comprehend your genuine objectives.

> *"The reward of deeds depends upon the intentions, and every person will receive the rewards according to what he has intended..." (Sahih Bukhari & Sahih Muslim)*

Muslims are required to pray five times a day with focus and obedience. Regardless of gender, many people frequently struggle with mental distractions during prayers. One of the nicest things you can hope for is to attain "khushu" (humility and concentration) in your prayers, which can be cultivated through mindfulness practice. Mindfulness enhances the depth and sincerity of prayers only if you are mentally present.

> *Allah (SWT) praises those with khushu (focus) during prayer: "Successful indeed are the believers, those who offer their Salah (prayers) with all solemnity and full submissiveness." (Quran 23:1-2)*

Mindfulness increases your awareness, making you more equipped to manage your thoughts. For instance, you might first notice feelings of impatience or a lack of gratitude and then consciously remind yourself to have patience and express gratitude to Allah (SWT).

> *The Prophet (PBUH) said, "To harbour good thoughts is part of well-practised worship." (Mishkat al Masabih)*

The goal of mindfulness is to live in the now. The present is where life happens! You are missing your life if you are not living in the here and now! Being mindful facilitates noticing the positive aspects of your surroundings. Concentrating on what you do have rather than what you lack might be beneficial. Being mindful helps you distinguish between thoughts that make you feel good and ones that make you feel bad. Insha'Allah, this will enable you to think more optimistically.

Recognising your blessings in the here and now is one benefit of living in the now and letting go of regrets from the past and anxieties for the future. Rather than whining about what you do not have, you start to feel grateful for your existence. This characterises a sincere Muslim. Your productivity will eventually increase as you notice more positive things around you. Furthermore, it goes without saying that the more you receive, the more grateful you are!

Due to your hectic schedule, you might frequently neglect to take care of yourself. Self-care includes your physical, mental, and spiritual well-being. By practising mindfulness as a detoxifying activity, you can deal with daily burnout and cleanse your mind. When you turn your attention from your racing thoughts to the here and now, you become more conscious of your needs. Therefore, you can take some time for yourself to unwind and clear your head after a demanding schedule.

Practical Steps for Spiritual Growth

Building a closer relationship with Allah (SWT) is necessary for a happy and meaningful life as a Muslim. It strengthens our faith, offers support in trying times, and promotes tranquillity and serenity. To strengthen this bond, you can establish a consistent prayer routine, perform your five daily prayers with sincerity and dedication, pray on time, and focus on the meaning of the words you recite.

It is also essential to practise dhikr and remember; cultivating a dhikr habit by repeating phrases or lines from the Quran or thinking about Allah's (SWT) qualities and benefits keeps our minds fixed on Him. We can gain a deeper understanding of Islam by attending Islamic lectures and classes and studying the Quran, Hadith, and the lives of the prophets. By expressing thanks and thinking back on Allah's (SWT) bounties on a daily basis, we might develop a sense of contentment with His divine design.

Our hearts are purified when we turn to Allah (SWT) in true repentance, ask for pardon, and try not to make the same mistakes twice.

Our love for Allah (SWT) is demonstrated by performing deeds of charity and generosity, such as providing financial support, donating our time, and offering assistance to those in need.

It is necessary to keep our mind focused on Allah (SWT) by remembering Him often, consulting Him while making decisions, and asking for His guidance. Joining online study groups such as the Online Islamic Institute can help you learn more. We can achieve great serenity and fulfilment and strengthen our relationship with Allah (SWT) by adhering to these guidelines.

Chapter Three

Morning Rituals for Spiritual Awakening

Islam greatly emphasises a person's morning routine since it establishes the tone for productivity, spiritual development, and general well-being. Islamic customs provide a whole manual for beginning the day, including moral precepts, physical regimens, and spiritual exercises that promote a well-rounded lifestyle. Let's explore the Islamic recommended time to start the day, based on the Hadith (sayings of the Prophet (PBUH)), the Quran, and the customs of the early Muslims.

Every Muslim should start a day with morning supplication. Starting your day with a morning dua (supplication) is not just a spiritual custom; it is a powerful practice that can significantly influence your day and life. Reciting a dua every morning can help us find serenity, focus, and thankfulness amidst the chaos of our everyday lives. The morning dua provides a time of peace and introspection before the day's responsibilities take over, acting as a spiritual anchor.

It is a technique that helps you start the day on a positive note by aligning your heart and mind with your aims, hopes, and appreciation. By bringing your goals and behaviours into alignment, these times of prayer and contemplation help you start the day on a positive note. Making a morning dua to begin your day enhances your relationship with Allah (SWT). This is an opportunity to express your thanks, anxieties, and hopes to build a stronger spiritual bond.

It is thought that the early morning hours, from 4:00am to 6:00am, are particularly potent since this is when the veil between the spiritual and the physical, or between human and divine consciousness, is the thinnest. Consequently, it is referred to as the Creator's hour and is a highly potent moment for setting goals for the upcoming day and reawakening our spirituality. To begin our day, a few morning duas are:

For Morning Remembrance:

> *"We have reached the morning, and at this very time unto Allah belongs all sovereignty, and all praise is for Allah. None has the right to be worshipped except Allah, alone, without partner, to Him belongs all sovereignty and praise and He is over all things omnipotent. My Lord, I ask You for the good of this day and the good of what follows it, and I take refuge in You from the evil of this day and the evil of what follows it. My Lord, I take refuge in You from laziness and senility. My Lord, I take refuge in You from torment in the Fire and punishment in the grave." (Quran 9:289)*

For Renewed Faith:

> *All praise is due to Allah, who gave us life after He took it from us, and unto Him is the resurrection. (Sahih Muslim)*

> *"O Allah, by your leave we have reached the morning, and by Your leave, we have reached the evening, by Your leave we live and die and unto You is our resurrection." (Ibn Majah)*

The morning dua acts as a lighthouse to help us navigate the chaos of our everyday lives. It creates a peaceful, reflective, and spiritually uplifting moment that sets the tone for a productive day. By including morning duas in your daily practice, you open the door to a transforming spiritual journey by bringing positivity, gratitude, and serenity into your life.

Acknowledging how much influence a morning prayer has on your days and lives every morning is important. It is a practice that brings tranquillity, purpose, and happiness into your daily life while also improving your spiritual well-being. Incorporate these potent morning duas into your daily routine to begin your journey and experience the life-changing effects of this practice.

Fajr Prayer: The Foundation of a Mindful Morning

One of the central tenets of Islam is the five daily prayers. Muslims can be distinguished from non-Muslims by salah (namaz), which is primarily a way to invoke Allah (SWT) and ask for His pleasure.

> *In the Holy Quran, Allah says: "Indeed, those who believe and do righteous deeds and establish prayer and give Zakah will have their reward with their Lord, and there will be no fear concerning them, nor will they grieve." (Quran 2:277)*

They are the highest of all responsibilities after our Shahaadatain (testimony of faith). As the Prophet (PBUH) stated, they will be the first deeds to be judged on the Day of Judgement.

> *"Indeed, the first deed by which a servant will be called to account on the Day of Resurrection is his Salah*

> *(prayers). If it is good, he is successful and triumphant, but if it is defective, he has failed and lost." (Tirmidhi)*

The pre-dawn Islamic prayer known as the Fajr is very important to Muslims all around the world. It starts the day with a prayer for Allah's guidance and blessings. One of the five required prayers in Islam is the Fajr prayer, which is said before dawn. Believers have a special place in their hearts for it because it marks the start of a new day full of gifts and chances for spiritual development.

That said, we ought to know that the Fajr prayer is granted special mentions and unique virtues in the Quran and the hadiths of the Prophet (PBUH). These merits are meant to motivate us to do our best to observe it and to depict missing it as a real misfortune worthy of regret and deep introspection.

> *In the Holy Quran, Allah Almighty says about the importance of Fajr prayer: "So establish the Prayer after the declining of the sun (from its zenith, for Dhuhr and then ASR) to the dusk of the night (Maghrib and then 'Isha) and the (Quranic) recitation of Fajr [prayer]. Indeed, the (Quranic) recitation of Fajr is witnessed." (Quran 17:78)*

The Fajr prayer has been highly valued and respected; in fact, 'Aishah (RA) recounted that the Prophet (PBUH) said:

> *"The two (sunnah) rakahs of Fajr are better than this world and all it contains." (Tirmidhi)*

> *Moreover, the Prophet (PBUH) said: Whoever prays the morning prayer in congregation then sits remembering*

Allah until the sun rises, then prays two units of prayer has the reward like that of Hajj and 'Umrah. (Tirmidhi)

Importance of starting the day with Fajr Salah and its spiritual benefits

For you as a Muslim, the Fajr prayer is not just a religious duty but an essential daily requirement. It helps establish the tone for the remainder of your day and strengthens your spiritual bond with Allah (SWT). You can begin your day with dedication and thankfulness to Allah (SWT) by rising early and performing Fajr, which lays the groundwork for awareness and spirituality in the coming hours. Islam places great importance on the Fajr prayer, said just before daybreak while everything is calm and quiet.

The Prophet (PBUH) said: "Whoever prays the two cool prayers (Asr and Fajr) will go to Paradise." (Sahih Bukhari)

Jundub ibn Abdullah (RA) reported the Prophet (PBUH) saying:

"He who performs the Fajr prayer will be under the protection of Allah. So beware, O son or daughter of Adam, that Allah does not call you to account for being absent from His protection for any reason." (Sahih Muslim)

There are physical and spiritual advantages to rising early for Fajr. It is common knowledge that rising early promotes physical well-being and lays the groundwork for an efficient day. It is a common misconception that meditation only takes an hour to keep you focused and serene, yet Islam incorporates meditation into daily life. We practise meditation by saying our five prayers a day. They fill your life with barakah (blessings) and noor (light) and continually remind you of Allah (SWT).

The following are some major spiritual advantages of rising early for Fajr prayer and offering it on time:

Love for Allah: It signifies adherence to the divine precepts. The core of the Islamic religion is submission to Allah's (SWT) will, which is demonstrated by the performance of the Fajr prayer.

Blessings: Offering your Fajr prayer on time is thought to bring you a wealth of blessings. The serenity and purity of the early morning hours are favourable for receiving blessings and spiritual connections.

Relationship with the Almighty: The Fajr prayer presents a unique chance for close, personal interaction with Allah (SWT). Early morning silence allows one to ponder, pray, and connect more deeply with the Creator.

Discipline: It takes commitment and discipline to get up early for Fajr prayers. Regular Fajr prayers build discipline that can be applied to other facets of life, such as productivity and self-control.

Enhanced productivity: Saying the Fajr prayer first thing in the morning creates a positive energy that lasts the entire day. It gives believers mental clarity and spiritual sustenance, empowering them to approach their responsibilities with resolve and focus.

Fulfilment of the first obligation of the day: Saying the Fajr prayer on time completes the first required act of devotion. This deepens one's commitment to Islam and lays the groundwork for carrying out other religious obligations.

Protection from evil: The Holy Prophet (PBUH) stressed the significance of saying the Fajr prayer in groups, asserting that those who do so are protected by Allah (SWT).

Here are various advantages and a happy message for individuals who recite the Fajr prayer every day. For Muslims to reap such immense rewards and blessings in this life and the next, they should always keep the following in mind.

Early risers have the advantage of having more time for yoga and physical activity, which keeps them mentally and physically fit. Aside from receiving a tonne of blessings and barakah, people who begin their days in the name of Allah (SWT) also tend to think optimistically, which can aid in mental tranquillity.

Last but not least, the Morning Prayer also encourages a healthy lifestyle, which is another somewhat subtle advantage. The night is meant for sleeping, and numerous academic studies demonstrate that those who work nights experience deteriorating health.

The Islamic lifestyle encourages going to bed late after Isha and waking up at the hour of Fajr. This helps us combat our innate tendencies towards lethargy and laziness and permits physical systems to return to normal.

Incorporating Dhikr and Quran recitation at dawn

In the Islamic context, "dhikr" means "remembrance" and refers to remembering Allah (SWT). Remembering Allah (SWT) is more beneficial in the morning and evening times than any other time.

Allah (SWT) tells us in the Quran: "O you who believe! Remember Allah with much remembrance." (Quran 33:41)

> *Our Prophet (PBUH) also told us: "He who remembers his Lord and he who does not are like the living and the dead." (Sahih Bukhari & Sahih Muslim)*

Reciting prayers or Arabic words aloud is a spiritual practice known as "dhikr," which Muslims perform to remember and honour Allah (SWT) or to offer blessings to the Holy Prophet (PBUH).

Dhikr also entails remembering Allah (SWT) before engaging in a great deal of other actions, such as when one wakes up in the morning, before beginning anything, before eating, before leaving the house, and before visiting different places.

The proper prayers for each situation have been taught to us by our Prophet (PBUH), and if we can repeat them with comprehension, then all we do will, hopefully, amount to remembering and worshipping Him. These can be learned with a little effort, but even if one is unable to recall the correct one, acknowledging Allah (SWT) and reciting the "Bismillah" constitutes dhikr and will bring blessings to all we do.

The benefits of remembering Allah (SWT) throughout the day are explained by the Messenger of Allah (PBUH) as if you remember Allah (SWT) in this life, He will remember you in the next and remember you wonderfully.

> *The Prophet said: "Allah says: 'I am just as my slave thinks I am, (i.e. I am able to do for him what he thinks I can do for him) and I am with him if He remembers Me. If he remembers Me in himself, I, too, remember him in Myself; and if he remembers Me in a group of people, I remember him in a group that is better than they; and if he comes one span nearer to Me, I go one cubit nearer to him; and if he comes one cubit nearer to Me, I go a distance of two outstretched arms nearer to him; and*

if he comes to Me walking, I go to him running"(Sahih Bukhari)

According to Aisha (RA), the Holy Prophet (PBUH) was committed to remembering Allah (SWT) at all times and in all circumstances. In our religion, numerous approved forms of dhikr are honourable and commendable; reciting inwardly means connecting with the words and reciting them honestly. Tafsir Marif-ul-Quran classified therein three types of inward recitation.

When a person focuses only on Allah (SWT) and His qualities in their heart, they are engaging in al-dhikr-al-khafiyy or dhikr of the heart. The second type occurs when the tongue is in tune with what is going on in his heart's innermost thoughts. The third type, which is the most desirable, is to be fully present in his heart and then to express it verbally using voice and tongue movements.

Reading the Quran is, in the end, the highest kind of dhikr. For every letter you read, you will receive ten awards. This award essentially serves as an example of the importance and proper place of the Quran in your life. Seeking the Barakah of the Quran is more valuable than working hard to raise our social standing or financial profits since, if done carelessly, without meaning, or in opposition to our life's goal, these things will pass away with us in this world and mean nothing in the next.

Attempt to establish a closer, more private, and exclusive relationship with the Book of Allah by reciting it first thing in the morning after the Fajr prayer and reflecting carefully and silently on its words. Then, make duas to ask for additional guidance and understanding of its contents.

The Quran itself refers to the recital of the Quran after the prayer of Fajr as something that "is witnessed" by Allah:

> *"Establish regular prayers – at the sun's decline till the darkness of the night, and the morning prayer and reading: for the prayer and reading in the morning carry their testimony."* (Quran 17:78)

The Quranic verse above clearly indicates that the pre-dawn hours are especially blessed because the angels witness the recitation of the Quran during the Fajr prayer. This is not because reciting it at dawn is the only time it is witnessed, nor is it because we will receive more credit for it in the Hereafter than if we recite it at other times.

Rather, reciting the Quran at dawn offers unique benefits as our minds are completely open to learning and reflecting on the meaning of the Quran before dawn because there are no outside distractions or sounds to disturb us. However, reading the Quran at any time is always accepted.

Establishing a Morning Routine of Gratitude and Reflection

Participating in a practice that reorganises your routines in ways that are fruitful and promote self-growth is a potent approach to establishing intention and offering a mindful roadmap for your day. That is the purpose of the morning routine. Read on to see how purposeful design can improve your day by establishing a morning ritual of gratitude and reflection by reading on.

Practising Shukr (thankfulness) for blessings and opportunities

Not only is gratitude the core of Islam, but it is also the secret of drawing success, wealth, harmony, and tranquillity into one's life. The two most significant tenets of Islam are gratitude (Shukr). As Muslims, we have an unending obligation to express gratitude to Almighty Allah

(SWT) for all of His favours. Not only is He the only Creator of this planet, but He is also the Most Merciful to all humanity. If we are grateful to him, we are believers; if not, we are unbelievers.

To love Allah (SWT) is to walk the road of gratitude (Shukr). The sole defence against unbelief need is Shukr. It is the remedy for melancholy and consumerism, as well as the inspiration to perform better the next day. Giving someone a thank you or expression of gratitude is essentially a way to return their generosity and honour the person who has shown us kindness and goodness. We should always be grateful to the Almighty Allah, the nicest of all, for everything.

In the Holy Quran, Allah Almighty says: "And remember! Your Lord caused to be declared: If you are grateful, I will add more unto you." (Quran 14:5-7)

We should be thankful for everything we have, including our health, riches, breath, family, friends, and everything else, no matter how small or large. Most significantly, though, we should be thankful that we are Muslims and that we come from the Prophet's (PBUH) Ummah. Allah (SWT) is pleased with people who express gratitude to Him for everything in their lives.

Gratitude purges your soul of the decaying layers of unfavourable feelings. It is the most powerful attitude there is. Perhaps it is the only one strong enough to free us from all these other negative feelings. Adopting a mindset (an attitude towards life) rooted in gratitude deactivates our nafs, such as low self-worth, envy, avarice, hatred, excessive ambition, laziness and arrogance. A great deal of unpleasant emotions are linked to a lack of thankfulness.

Shukr is a thoughtful meditation on the innumerable blessings the Creator has bestowed upon you. This deliberate act of gratitude starts a process of internal transformation in which negative emotions give way to feelings of gratitude and optimism. Shukr enables you to perceive the beauty and richness all around you and see the world through a lens of appreciation.

How can one give thanks to Allah (SWT) for all of His blessings? His thankfulness should meet all the requirements, which include gratitude from the heart, gratitude from the speech, and gratitude from the body.

> *May Allah have pity on Ibn al-Qayyim, who said: "Gratitude may be in the heart, in submission and humility; on the tongue, in praise and acknowledgement; and in the physical faculties, by means of obedience and submission?" (Madarij al-Salikin)*

Ways to Practise Shukr in Islam

There are some ways of following, for which we should be grateful (Shukr) Allah Almighty (SWT).

Say Alhamdulillah frequently: This reminds us of the source of all blessings and happiness in this life; uttering this statement repeatedly helps. We remain modest because we attribute all good deeds to Allah (SWT).

> *The Holy Prophet (PBUH) said: "Allah is pleased with His servant if when he eats something he thanks Allah for it, and when he drinks something he thanks Allah for it." (Sahih Muslim)*

Fall in prostration while receiving blessings from Allah: Whenever we receive blessings from the Almighty Allah (SWT), we should fall in prostration (Sajdah). When our beloved Prophet (PBUH) received something nice, He would also bow down to thank Allah Almighty (SWT).

Be patient and grateful during a difficult time: Our capacity for thankfulness is tested when we encounter a challenging situation. Allah wants to know how appreciative we are when we experience illness or injury when we lose our job or a loved one.

> *The Prophet (PBUH) said, "How wonderful is the case of a Believer! There is good for him in whatever happens to him -and none, apart from him, enjoys this blessing."*
> *(Sahih Muslim)*

This implies that there is always ease following adversity and that those who persevere through adversity and remain grateful to Allah (SWT) will reap enormous rewards.

Be sociable and avoid being overly particular: Ungratefulness, haughtiness, selfishness and insensitivity to other people's preferences can hinder your ability to accommodate and connect with them. Embrace comfort in all circumstances, and you will discover gratitude.

Remember to keep your expectations low: Always show admiration for those less fortunate than you or who lack what you have, and always give thanks to Allah (SWT) for what you have rather than comparing yourself to others. Many people lack even the basic necessities and blessings, so you should be grateful to Allah (SWT) for what you have. The best way to appease Allah is to be grateful. Thank you, Allah (SWT).

> *The Holy Prophet (PBUH) said: "Look at those people who have less than you and never look at those who have more grants than you; this will ensure that you will not depreciate Allah's favours" (Sahih Muslim)*

Your life will alter if you adopt an attitude of gratitude towards Allah (SWT). Enjoying the benefits bestowed by his Lord, one will give thanks to Him for those blessings and praise for enabling him to be counted among those who give thanks. Thus, constantly be humble and thank Allah (SWT) for His favours.

Setting positive intentions (niyyah) for the day ahead

Intentions, or "niyyah" as they are known in Arabic, are important concepts in Islam. As a matter of fact, intentions are the foundation of every action in Islam and a major factor in establishing the moral worth and consequence of that action. Niyyah is the inner motivation that propels us forward and moulds our conduct. It is the deliberate decision we make before starting any kind of activity, no matter how big or tiny. It is, in essence, the rationale for our actions. Islam places great significance on niyyah, which is based primarily on the Quran and Hadith.

> *In the Quran, Allah says: "Take provisions, but indeed, the best provision is Taqwa (piety, righteousness). So fear Me, you of understanding." (Quran 2:197)*

Our acts are evaluated based on their motivations as much as their looks. Therefore, in Islam, it is crucial to have a true and moral goal.

> *The Prophet (PBUH) further emphasises the importance of niyyah. He said: "Actions are but by intention, and every man shall have only that which he intended." (Sahih Bukhari)*

21st-century living is chaos. We can easily become overwhelmed with never-ending to-do lists, nonstop communications, and insufficient hours in a day to complete everything. It makes sense that we frequently feel pressured and worn out. Thus, what are some ways to simplify our lives while still having direction and purpose?

Understanding how to set intentions can help you create structure and tranquillity in your daily life. Intentions are strong instruments that can help you prioritise and concentrate on the things that are really important in life.

Try to develop the skill of establishing your intentions for the day before you even get out of bed. It strengthens your muscles of gratitude and self-awareness. Establishing intentions also aids in focusing and staying focused during the day. A more confident mind is concentrated. Every morning, you will be more focused and productive if you have a purpose for the day. This will make your days happier and more productive overall.

Begin your day with "Bismillah" (in the name of Allah), invoking His blessings and reminding yourself that all actions are for His sake. Make dua, asking Allah (SWT) for guidance and strength to fulfil your intentions with sincerity, patience, and gratitude. Be specific about your intentions, such as praying salah on time, being patient and kind to family, or seeking and applying knowledge. Throughout the day, take moments to renew and remind yourself of your niyyah, especially before starting new tasks or when feeling distracted. This practice helps maintain focus and spiritual mindfulness.

By consciously setting positive intentions at the start of the day, Muslims can transform their everyday actions into acts of worship, drawing closer to Allah (SWT) and earning His pleasure and rewards. This practice enhances one's spiritual life and brings peace, purpose, and blessings to daily endeavours.

Chapter Four

Daily Quranic Reflections

Islam values the Quran highly because it provides a comprehensive framework for morality, behaviour, and belief. The Quran serves as a material and spiritual roadmap for people of all social classes and communities and throughout human history in all nations.

It imparts universal lessons. It illuminates the route to the afterlife and the spirit of man. Believers achieve spiritual fulfilment and comfort by drawing daily inspiration and guidance from the Quran.

> *Allah says about the Quran: "There certainly has come to you from Allah a light and a clear Book through which Allah guides those who seek His pleasure to the ways of peace, brings them out of darkness and into light by His Will, and guides them to the Straight Path." (Quran 5:15-16)*

Moreover, Allah (SWT) makes apparent the significance of the Quran in our day-to-day lives:

> *"This is a blessed Book we have revealed. So follow it and be mindful ˹of Allah˺, so you may be shown mercy."*
> *(Quran 6:155)*

All people can find Allah's message in the Holy Quran. It instructs people on proper behaviour and towards living in this world correctly. The afterlife is also discussed in the Book of Allah. It informs us that Allah (SWT) has prepared Hell for the wicked and Paradise for the righteous.

The Quran promotes worship of the one Allah (SWT), who creates and sustains humanity. The book condemns wrongdoers and forbids individuals from doing evil. It includes historical prophets' accounts and illustrations of good and terrible individuals. The Qur'an counsels people to treat others with kindness and respect. It instructs individuals on how to live in harmony and peace.

Muslims use the Quran as a guideline because it contains tales of prophets and believers meant to convey wisdom and govern daily activities. Reciting the Qur'an daily helps one's faith in Allah (SWT) grow, providing calmness to the heart and soul and serenity throughout life's challenges. Furthermore, every letter repeated reaps great benefits, shields believers from evil powers, and pleads in their favour on the Day of Judgement.

Importance of Quranic Recitation and Tadabbur (Reflection)

Millions of people worldwide find spiritual enlightenment, direction, and healing in the Quran, the sacred book of Islam. Daily recitation is not only required by religion but also has many material and immaterial advantages. Reciting the holy book every day has numerous benefits for your heart and intellect.

Every area of our lives requires direction, and the Quran provides the best direction. It serves as a guide for daily living, giving us comprehensive instructions on how to live a decent and happy life, covering everything from little things to significant issues pertaining to society, worship, or personal problems.

In fact, Muslims can better grasp the mysteries of their cosmos by studying the Quran. The Quran also aids in their understanding of the universe's governing laws and the mysteries of creation. Meditating on the Quran can give you ideal answers to the existential issues that generally plague you. To put it plainly, you can find the answers to queries about the meaning of life, the nature of man, the afterlife, and the way to true happiness and peace.

Daily recitation of the Holy Quran has spiritual advantages but can also aid understanding and memorising with practice. Repetition and memorisation test the brain's memory while helping it retain information.

Repetitive activity is an effective learning strategy that helps people remember things, including the important lessons found in the Quran. The sacred book of Islam is a foreign language to many Muslims because it is written in Arabic. Devout Muslims can become more intuitive learners of Allah's message and closer to their faith through daily recitation.

With each letter of the Quran you read, you will reap more rewards. Consequently, you will grow your scale of good deeds in the Hereafter and earn you greater rewards. This means the Quran benefits you both in this world and the Hereafter.

Anybody's life can be illuminated by the Quran, which points the way to the light. If you recite the book daily, you will stay on the straight path and be motivated to perform good deeds. The individual whose heart is tied to the book of Allah (SWT) will naturally avoid sins and accept the laws and lessons revealed in that book. It has a magical impact similar to prayer.

The Quran has the power to heal all ailments and sufferings, whether mental, physical, or spiritual. Reciting the Quran can help you eliminate known and unknowable annoyances. It increases our faith and shines a light of faith on the heart. For this reason, memorising and reciting the Quran is essential to receiving Allah's (SWT) forgiveness and healing.

> *In the Quran, Allah says: "And We send down from the Quran that which is healing and mercy for the believers, and it does not increase the wrongdoers except in loss."*
> *(Quran 17:82)*

Furthermore, the genuine hadiths tell of people being with the people they love on the Day of Resurrection. And we shall all want the right companion to experience Allah Almighty's (SWT) mercy on that final day.

Thus, if we love the Quran, we will be among the people of the Quran and the virtuous. Our dear Prophet (PBUH) received revelations from the Quran. The Prophet (PBUH) spoke of its manners and humanity's need for them.

Thus, the Quran is an eternal beacon of illumination. In every regard, it is an ideal approach and manner of living. It possesses an unmatchable force that cannot be resisted. It is the wellspring of knowledge and the basis of faith.

The best remedy for any ailment is found in the Quran. It is the indestructible string of Allah (SWT). It is the actual straight way and a sensible reminder. If you want to communicate with Allah (SWT), pray and ask for guidance. If you want to hear from Allah (SWT), read the Quran. No one can love you more than Allah (SWT), the one who made you. Anyone who reads the Quran knows Allah's mercy, which extends to forgiving his servants' misdeeds with just one tear of repentance.

Since the Holy Quran contains the words and messages of Allah (SWT) to his followers, it is the most important book in a Muslim's life. The advantages and virtues readers get from reading this book until the end demonstrate its significance. These advantages apply to both this life and the Hereafter.

Finding tranquillity (Sakinah) through recitation and understanding of the Quran

The quality or condition of being at ease, content, and free from tension and suffering is known as tranquillity. The term "tranquillity" can be found in a wide range of texts, from religious writings where it describes the peace of the body, mind, and consciousness on the path to liberation to a variety of documents where its meaning is closely linked to interaction with the natural world.

It is Allah (SWT) who bestows peace and steadiness on believers' hearts, enabling them to grow in their faith beyond what they already possess. The forces of the earth and heavens belong only to Allah, who uses them to support any of His slaves that He pleases. Allah (SWT) is Wise in providing support and aid since He is aware of the interests of His people.

> *Allah says: "It is He who sent down tranquillity into the hearts of the believers that they would increase in faith along with their [present] faith. And to Allah belong the soldiers of the heavens and the earth, and ever is Allah Knowing and Wise." (Quran 48:4)*

Sakinah, an extremely semantically rich Arabic phrase, means inner peace, quiet, serenity, tranquillity, and repose. As a result, it refers to a condition of inner being marked by immense tranquillity, perfect calm, a sense of inner security, etc.

Al-Bara' Ibn 'Azib reported: A man was reciting Surat al-Kahf when an animal became unsettled in his barn. He could not see anything because of a mist or cloud covering him.

> *The Prophet (PBUH) heard him mention that, and he responded: "Continue reciting, for it was calm which descended with the Quran, or for the Quran." (Sahih Muslim)*

Finding Sakinah through the recitation and understanding of the Quran is a multifaceted journey that involves regular recitation, deep understanding, reflection, and application of its teachings. This process nurtures the soul and brings a profound sense of inner peace and tranquillity, aligning one's heart and mind with the divine wisdom of Allah (SWT).

Extracting spiritual insights (Tafsir) from verses relevant to daily life

Tafsir, which comes from the Arabic word "fasara," signifies "interpretation" or "exegesis." It alludes to the academic project of clarifying the subtleties and meanings found in the passages of the Quran. Tafsir thoroughly examines the historical background, linguistic features, legal ramifications, and spiritual components of the Quran. It acts as a link between the divine message contained in the Quran and human reason.

"Tafsir" describes the academic analysis and interpretation of the passages of the Quran. Its goal is to clarify the meanings, contexts, and implications of Quranic passages, providing an understanding of the divine wisdom and intended messages that Allah (SWT) conveys via His revelations.

Understanding Tafsir in daily life will help us reflect spiritually; it can also be a tool for introspection and contemplation. By considering the meanings of the Quranic verses, Muslims can strengthen their relationship with Allah (SWT) and discover a deeper sense of meaning and purpose in life.

Reading Tafsir can motivate Muslims to fight for social justice and human rights. Muslims can study the passages in the Quran that support justice, equality, and compassion to become more proficient change agents in their local and global communities.

Muslims can also improve their moral and personal character with the aid of tafsir. Muslims can learn how to live an ethically responsible, compassionate, and honest life by studying the Quran and its interpretations. Tafsir can also be used to encourage communication and understanding between different religions. Muslims can have meaningful discussions and cooperate towards shared objectives with individuals of other religions by learning the meanings of the Quranic passages.

Tafsir Types

- Tafsir Bil-Ma'thur: Derived from early scholars' interpretations and prophetic traditions.

- Tafsir Al-Tafsir: Extensive works that provide in-depth interpretation by combining linguistic, historical, theological, and legal studies.

- Tafsir Bil-Ra'y: Within the confines of Islamic doctrine, derived from both academic and personal reasoning.

Tafsir illuminates the breadth and depth of the divine word and acts as guiding light for those who study the Quran. It is a priceless tool for Muslims who want to learn more about the Quran because of its complex methodologies, historical evolution, and current relevance. Through our interaction with Tafsir, we can connect the timeless teachings of the Quran and our modern lives, gaining direction, inspiration, and spiritual development.

To extract spiritual insights (Tafsir) from Quranic verses relevant to daily life, start with sincere intention and humility. Choose verses that resonate with your current challenges, focusing on themes like patience, gratitude, and justice. Use reputable Tafsir resources like Tafsir Ibn Kathir and Tafsir Al-Jalalayn to understand the context and deeper meanings.

Reflect on how the teachings apply and make practical changes accordingly. For example, "Indeed, Allah is with the patient" (Quran 2:153) encourages patience and trust in Allah (SWT) during hardships, fostering resilience and inner peace.

Implementing Quranic Teachings into Daily Actions

Reciting the verses from the Holy Quran is one thing; applying its precepts to day-to-day activities is another and no less significant. It takes a correct comprehension of the Holy Quran to apply its lessons in day-to-day living. The Holy Quran is more than just a compendium of laws or information; it also emphasises laying a solid foundation in one's heart and fostering and bolstering one's faith and spirituality. It can be said that the Quran offers immense consolation and encouragement in all aspects of life, regardless of the challenges one may encounter.

The most crucial thing for Muslims to accomplish is to incorporate the lessons found in the Holy Quran into their daily lives. The Quran contains the actual accounts of ancient communities and customs. We are presented with these tales to comprehend reality. We must have faith in Allah (SWT), and the essential quality that gives us courage and strength is His Mighty Power.

The Holy Quran contains a plethora of instances that we might use to support our Hidaya (right path). Embracing the lessons of the Quran into one's daily life is a way to achieve inner peace, satisfaction, and a closer relationship with God, in addition to being a show of devotion.

Applying Quranic wisdom to relationships, work, and personal development

Applying Quranic wisdom to relationships, work, and personal development can profoundly enhance various aspects of life. Here is how to integrate this wisdom:

In Islam, forming wholesome relationships is very important. For Allah (SWT), we are commanded by our faith to cultivate solid and wholesome relationships based on love, respect, and compassion for others. Our lives are significantly impacted by the intimate interactions we have with our loved ones.

These relationships provide emotional support, company, and a feeling of belonging. They support, uplift, and inspire us as we face life's obstacles. Love and kindness are the cornerstones of any thriving partnership. Islam strongly emphasises developing these traits in all relationships, including with friends, family, and community.

Comprehending the meaning of Quranic verses regarding relationships can offer significant direction on fostering wholesome and satisfying relationships with others. The teachings of the Quran provide direction on virtues like forgiveness, kindness, empathy, and respect that can help people forge closer bonds with their loved ones, friends, and neighbours.

> *"And We have not sent you, [O Muhammad], except as a mercy to the worlds" (Quran 21:107)*

> *"The best among you are those who have the best manners and character."(Sahih Bukhari)*

Whatever the Almighty chooses for us to have in our lives is balanced and ideal. The wisdom of Allah's (SWT) knowledge of why we face hardships is occasionally shown to us, but we must wait for hindsight to recognise it. As believers, we realise that whatever Allah (SWT) chooses for us is the best, especially as we learn more about our deen. We understand that everything in life is a test, good and terrible, agreeable and disagreeable. As a result, despite our challenges, we should never give up hope.

> *"O you who have believed, fear Allah and be with those who are true" (Quran 9:119)*

The Quran is frequently referred to as the supreme manual for living. It offers precise instructions on how to lead an upright and moral life. It serves as a moral compass for Muslims by providing a moral framework complete with prohibitions and mandates. People who follow the teachings of the Quran strive to live their lives according to the will of God, which is essential to their spiritual development.

The Quran exhorts people to work towards moral and spiritual growth in themselves. It acts as a manual for character development, inspiring believers to face their weaknesses, practise self-control, and focus on their own development.

> *"And by the soul and He who proportioned it and inspired it with discernment of its wickedness and its righteousness" (Quran 91:7-8)*

It is our duty as Muslims to constantly work towards bettering ourselves in both our spiritual and material lives. While our dear Prophet (PBUH) counselled us to be the best versions of ourselves, Allah (SWT) urges us to grow and develop. It is even more important for us to take charge of our personal development in a world full of obstacles and a pressing demand for change.

We must better ourselves in many ways, such as by embracing more Islamic practices or elevating secular facets of our lives to assist us in navigating the difficulties of this life and carrying out our Islamic duties. This is because accepting personal transformation not only helps ourselves but also the environment in which we live.

In summary, Muslims can find a rich and varied supply of spiritual sustenance in the Quran. Its verses inform, inspire, console, and guide all who read them. Its contribution to spiritual development goes beyond personal development, including building a closer bond with God and a sense of fellowship among Muslims. The Quran's lasting impact on believers' lives confirms that it is the best source of instruction for Muslims pursuing spiritual and personal advancement.

Strengthening faith (Iman) through Quranic contemplation

In general, our Iman is not strong, and occasionally, we might stray from the right path due to our ignorance, especially when it comes to how we can better our self-esteem and fight against our inner desires and ambitions.

To strengthen your faith, rely solely on Allah (SWT) and adhere to Islamic teachings. Observe and comprehend the Quran, as it holds the answers to your problems. Reciting the Quran will strengthen your Iman, and a deeper grasp of the Quran will increase your faith in Allah (SWT).

Reading the words and teachings of Allah (SWT) will bring you closer to Him. Additionally, when you read the Quran with all of your heart and comprehend the meanings behind each verse, you will feel the passages' extraordinary power. Thus, your trust in Allah (SWT) will increase.

Allah mentioned this benefit in the Quran: "The believers are only those who, when Allah is mentioned, feel a fear in their hearts and when His Verses are recited unto them, they increase their Faith; and they put their trust in their Lord (Alone)." (Quran 8:2)

You will find that the Quran has a profoundly calming and consoling effect on your heart and soul. It nourishes hearts and souls, dispels uncertainty and concern, points you in the direction of righteousness, and enlightens your heart.

It is the responsibility of every Muslim to learn and memorise the Quran. It enables pious adherents of the faith to obtain benefits from Allah, inner serenity, and divine acceptance. By memorising its verses, devout Muslims can reach their maximum potential in terms of growth, learning, and improvement.

Connecting with the Creator is guaranteed when you read the Quran. Knowing who Allah is and who you are will determine your strength in your Iman or religion. We all go on a trip when we read the Quran, and it is throughout that journey—which involves reading in a language you can comprehend—that you reflect on the wisdom Allah (SWT) provides. Until you take that journey, you will not reap its benefits. When you recognise your connection with your creator, you will have strength in your Iman.

As you study the Quran, you will naturally discover that Allah (SWT) provides many solutions to your life issues.

The most significant advantage of reading the Quran is that it will make you feel closer to your Creator and give you the impression that He is speaking to you. You will discover that Allah (SWT) knows many ideas you consistently think about. He provides you with a reading answer for such issues.

Chapter Five

Dhikr & Remembrance of Allah (SWT)

Islam is a way of life rather than just a religion with worship and rituals. It offers guidance to individuals in every sphere of life. One of the most fundamental ideas of Islam is dependence on Allah (SWT) for all aspects of life, asking Him for strength, assistance, and guidance because He is the one who created the entire world and is ultimately in charge of it.

This dependence on Allah (SWT) is achieved by constant recall and repeated prayer, where dhikr and dua come in. In Islam, dhikr (remembrance of Allah) and dua (supplication) are two comparable and highly significant forms of devotion.

Dhikr is a valuable ibadah that promotes spiritual health, peace, and heart softening. We are commanded to engage in the Dhikr of Allah as part of our spiritual practice.

> *The person who remembers Allah is like alive, whereas, not remembering Him is like dead (Bukhari and Muslim). The Prophet (PBUH) told us to keep the tongue wet with Dhikr (Tirmidhi)*

The Arabic word Dhikr means "remembrance" or "mention," is Adhkar in plural. However, in a religious context, it refers to remembering and mentioning Allah (SWT); it is simply worship, which is the act of praising Allah (SWT) with your heart and lips. Some of the most common phrases you may hear are "SubhanAllah," "Alhamdulillah," and "Allahu Akbar".

Each has a specific significance, but you can repeat them whenever and as many times as you want to reap the wonderful benefits. Additionally, there are dhikr (or Adhkar) unique to particular circumstances, events, and occasions. Adhkar is designated times for the morning, evening, bedtime, wake-up, after prayers (Salah), inside and outside the home. Let's look at this in detail.

Benefits of Dhikr and Its Role in Mindfulness

Reciting the name of Allah (SWT) aloud is a practice known as dhikr. It has significant psychological advantages that can improve your mental and emotional health. Despite having a strong spiritual foundation, it has important benefits for mental health that transcend beyond spirituality.

Some parts of the brain become active and engaged when practising Adhkar/remembrance on a daily basis. As a result, there is an increase in bio-electrical flow in certain neuronal groups inside the brain. This overflow causes new neurons to fire, activating more brain regions. As a result, the brain starts growing. When one practices dhikr, the brain begins to reveal fresh interpretations, viewpoints, and commentary that it had not previously employed.

Studies on the mental health advantages of participating in Islamic commemoration rituals demonstrate significant effects on people's mental health. Dhikr therapy is an Islamic-based mindfulness practice that is a potent tool for improving general well-being and spiritual healing. Regular dhikr practices help people develop heightened awareness and mindfulness, which helps them concentrate on the here and now and forge strong spiritual connections.

Dhikr is a type of mindfulness practice that calls for complete attention to the present moment. Concentrating on the recitation and the message underlying the words can lessen the effect of unfavourable thoughts about the past or future. Being attentive makes it simpler to focus and think clearly, facilitating doing daily chores with purpose and clarity.

Dhikr practice, then, offers psychological advantages that go beyond simple recitation and encompass a whole mental health strategy that incorporates spirituality, mindfulness, as well as emotional wellbeing. People who consistently participate in dhikr might undergo significant changes in their mental and emotional states, ultimately resulting in a higher level of serenity and contentment.

Elevating the heart (Qalb) through constant remembrance of Allah (SWT)

Your inner self is the more significant aspect of your "persona". The Quran refers to this inner self as the heart, or qalb. Dhikr is to the heart and soul what water is to fish. Thus, we must always remember our Lord and engage in dhikr to nourish our souls.

Muslims aim to focus on deepening their relationship with Allah (SWT) and cleansing their hearts from worldly distractions by frequently participating in dhikr.

Repeating certain verses or Allah's names and traits aloud will cause you to reflect on their meaning and recognise both Allah's (SWT) ultimate authority and your own limitations. This will positively impact your heart and strengthen your relationship with God.

"Verily, in the remembrance of Allah do hearts find rest."
(Quran 13:28)

"Whosoever shows enmity to someone devoted to Me, I shall be at war with him. My servant draws not near to Me with anything more loved by Me than the religious duties I have enjoined upon him, and My servant continues to draw near to Me with supererogatory works so that I shall love him. When I love him, I am his hearing with which he hears, his seeing with which he sees, his hand with which he strikes and his foot with which he walks. Were he to ask [something] of Me, I would surely give it to him, and were he to ask Me for refuge, I would surely grant him it. I do not hesitate about anything as much as I hesitate about [seizing] the soul of My faithful servant: he hates death, and I hate hurting him." (Sahih Bukhari)

The foregoing hadith summarises that we can win Allah's affection and attention by completing supererogatory deeds (nafil). Of course, this is done after performing/fulfilling the obligatory acts (Fard). Thus, when performing these supererogatory activities, it is important to do so sincerely and with love rather than as an anomaly or merely as a ritual or routine. This way, when you perform the Dhikr of Allah with love, Allah (SWT) reciprocates with even more love.

People look for peace amid the rush and bustle of contemporary life, where stress and anxiety are commonplace. Many people find solace in a variety of pursuits, including mindfulness, meditation, and hobbies. On the other hand, the deep wellspring of inner serenity for millions of Muslims worldwide is the memory of Allah, the Almighty in Islam.

Dhikr possesses a wonderful power to instil a sense of calm and inner serenity. It relaxes the soul and calms the heart, especially when tension or worry is high. Because dhikr is repetitive, individuals can centre themselves and find comfort in their beliefs. Remembering Allah (SWT) is a timeless and universal source of consolation that comforts hearts looking for relief from life's hardships. People who practise dhikr not only gain the psychological advantages of mindfulness but also strengthen their spiritual bond with the Creator and discover everlasting serenity in remembering Allah (SWT).

Dhikr and Mindfulness in Daily Life

Dhikr is a practice that can considerably improve mindfulness in daily life. It offers a deep spiritual and mental foundation that cultivates a sense of presence and connectivity with the Divine. As you perform dhikr throughout the day, keep the following in mind:

- **Heartfelt Recitation**: Say the dhikr aloud with sincerity, allowing Allah's (SWT) memory to linger profoundly in your soul.

- **Focused Intentions**: As you recite dhikr, direct your thoughts towards the Divine and allow your thoughts to revolve around a spiritual connection.

- **Environmental Awareness**: When practising dhikr, take note of your surroundings, centre yourself in the here and now, and recognise the wonders of creation.

- **Breathing Consciously**: Align your breathing with the dhikr's rhythmic recitation, combining spiritual contemplation with deliberate breathing exercises.

Through these practices, dhikr transforms into a tool that improves everyday mindfulness while fostering a deep spiritual connection that calms and centres your mental and emotional health.

Practising various forms of Dhikr (e.g., Tasbih, Tahmid, Takbir)

Below is a brief list of dhikr/remembrances that you can include in your day. The intention is for these lovely affirmations to the Creator to flow effortlessly from your lips and your heart.

- **Tasbih, Tahmid, Takbir**

SubhanAllah (33 times "glory be to Allah"), Alhamdulillah (33 times "praise be to Allah), Allahu Akbar (34 times "Allah is the greatest") can be recited after Salah and before you go to bed/sleep.

Reward: Although easy to utter with our tongues, on the Day of Judgement, they will be heavy on the scales. They remove sins and garner unparalleled rewards. They cultivate the trees and plants of Paradise, and are a protection from the Hellfire.

> *The Messenger of Allah said: "Indeed what you remember of Allah's Glory (by uttering) tasbiḥ, takbir, tahlil and taḥmid, gather around the Throne of Allah, buzzing like bees, mentioning to Allah the person who uttered them. Do you not wish to have someone who mentions you by Him?" (Ibn Majah)*

- **Astaghfirullah**

("I seek Allah's forgiveness")

Reward: You shall be shielded from the wrath of Allah. Allah (SWT) tells the tale of Prophet Nuh 'alayhi'l-salam (PBUH) in Surah Nuh, ayah 10–12. He also tells how he told his people to ask Allah (glorified and exalted be He) for forgiveness. All they had to do was chant "Astagfirullah," and Allah would provide them plenty of rain, double their wealth and offspring, and provide them with rivers and gardens in paradise.

> *"And said, 'Ask forgiveness of your Lord Indeed, He is ever a Perpetual Forgiver. He will send [rain from] the sky upon you in [continuing] showers. And give you increase in wealth and children and provide for you gardens and provide for you rivers."* (Quran 71: 10-12)

- **SubhanAllah or SubhanAllah wa bihamdihi**

("I praise Allah (or All praise if to Allah) above all attributes that do not suit His Majesty.")

Reward: By reciting this dhikr in Paradise, a tree will be planted for you. Hadith relates that whoever says this 100 times a day, his/her sins will be forgiven even if they were as much as the foam of the sea (Bukhari)

- **La hawla wa la quwwata illa billah**

("There is no power or might except (by) Allah.")

Reward: Those who often use this remembrance will enter through a special door in Paradise.

> *Qais bin Saad bin 'Ubadah narrated that his father offered him to the Prophet (PBUH) to serve him. He said: "So the Prophet (PBUH) passed by me, and I had just performed Salah, so he poked me with his foot and said: 'Should I not direct you to a gate from the gates of Paradise?' I said: 'Of course.' He (PBUH) said: There is no might or power except with Allah (La ḥawla wa la quwwata illa billah)." (Tirmidhi)*

Use these Adhkar (supplications) frequently and deliberately to seek blessings and be in Allah's (SWT) presence. Recite them to your Creator, and He will be by your side no matter what.

Incorporating Dhikr into Daily Routines and Activities

Cultivating a state of spiritual presence (hudur) in everyday tasks

Our lives are transformed by presence because it keeps us in the here and now. It includes the mind, body, and spirit and transcends beyond physical presence. It entails accepting the present moment, letting go of control, and having faith in how things will work out.

We may break through the delusion of separation and establish a connection with the universal energy that binds all creation through presence. This practice lets us enjoy life's small pleasures through inner peace and mental calmness.

In Islam, this kind of situation is called "Hudur" when the heart is away from all else; it is present with Allah (SWT). The only way for the slave to be in the presence of Allah (SWT) is by one of His Beautiful Names, which also preserves a flawless condition of spiritual civility.

Without calming your soul, you cannot become more aware of Allah's (SWT) presence. "Hurry is the great enemy of the spiritual life." For you to hear Allah (SWT) clearly, you need time and distance. Allah (SWT) is left behind when we are constantly on the go, rushing from task to task while wearing headphones, checking emails, the TV, etc. Make space for this connection; as indicated, the morning is the best time.

The Power of Remembering Allah (SWT)

Allah (SWT) reminds us of His boundless gifts and benefits, unending support, and the boundless goodness He provides, such as safety and security, calm and serenity, harmony and enjoyment, liberty and delight, and joy and pleasure.

When you remember Allah (SWT), you are with Him and linked to Him. This remembering combines the words on your tongue with your heart and mind. When you sense a connection to Allah (SWT), you will always get consolation and enduring delight from your Lord. Even if it feels like the entire world is closing in on you, shutting its doors, and shrouding you in darkness, you will experience a light that fills your heart.

Keep Allah (SWT) in mind, and you will be with him. Your heart will experience calm and serenity. Your faith will grow, your heart and mind will be at ease, and your confidence, assurance, and trust will be reinforced.

In the tale of the little child and the king, there was a little child who was the only one to firmly believe in and have faith in Allah (SWT). The ruler of the day ordered his soldiers to take the youngster to a tall mountain and throw him from the top if he did not abandon his faith and doubt in Allah (SWT) since he wanted to kill the boy. The child then recited the dua:

> *"O Allah, take care of them for me however you want to."*
> *(Sahih Muslim)*

As the troops took the child up the mountain, the mountain began to tremble, and the troops were killed. Unharmed, the youngster went back to the king. The monarch then ordered his men to drag him out to sea and threaten him once more, demanding He abandon his faith or be thrown into the water. The boy recited the same dua. The boat overturned, and while the others perished, the boy survived. He returned to the king once more. And so the tale continues.

From this narrative, we learn that the youngster could accomplish anything because he firmly believed in Allah (SWT) and his might. He also knew that Allah (SWT) was watching over him and trusted him to keep him safe.

Therefore, remembering Allah (SWT) deepens our relationship with Him, boosts our confidence in Him, and deepens our trust in Him—especially during difficult and trying times. Thus, remembering and pleading with Allah (SWT) in the morning and evening, praying, and engaging in other similar deeds will deepen your relationship with him and enshroud you in protection.

Chapter Six

Mindful Eating and Nutrition

Nutrition can significantly impact our bodies, minds, and general well-being. Sometimes, indulging in our favourite comfort foods can be a healthy element of self-care, but if it becomes a habit, it may be something to look into. Altering our eating habits, rather than just what we consume, can enhance our enjoyment of food. Enjoying the pleasure of eating more consciously is the goal of mindful eating, not dieting or following rules.

> *Allah has commanded the believers as He has commanded His Messengers by saying: 'O Messengers! Eat of the good things, and do good deeds.' (Quran 23:51)*

Keeping a present-moment awareness of the food and liquids you put in your body is known as mindful eating. It entails paying attention to your body's cues regarding flavour, enjoyment, and fullness, as well as how the meal makes you feel. Making decisions when eating mindfully enables one to choose foods that will please and nourish the body. However, since various eating experiences exist, it opposes "judging" one's eating habits. As we become more conscious of our eating patterns, we may work to modify our behaviour for the good of both the environment and ourselves.

You can learn to appreciate your food and the eating experience by being mindful of your feelings. At the same time, you eat, including the flavours and textures of each mouthful, your body's signals of hunger and fullness, and how different foods affect your mood and energy levels.

Making conscious meal choices might help you digest food more effectively, feel fuller after eating less, and make better eating decisions in the future. Additionally, it might assist you in breaking bad eating and food-related habits. Let's take a look at what Islam says about this.

Concept of Halal and Tayyib in Islamic Dietary Guidelines

The term "Halalan Tayyiban" describes the process of producing food that is both pure and wholesome (Tayyib) and Halal (permissible). It covers food production's safety, nutrition, hygiene, quality, and authenticity, ensuring that the finished product is not only acceptable but of the highest calibre and advantageous for ingestion.

"And eat of the things which Allah has provided for you, lawful (Halal) and good (Tayyib), and fear Allah in Whom you believe." (Quran 5:88)

Abu Bakr (RA) narrated that The Prophet Muhammad (PBUH) said: "That body will not enter Paradise which has been nourished with Haram." (Bayhaqi)

For Muslims, worship—that is, adoration of Allah Almighty—must be the cornerstone of every deed. According to Sharia law, eating is a kind of worship with specific rituals and laws. According to the Holy Quran, eating should be Tayyib rather than just Halal. Let's explore.

> *Allah says in the Quran: "O mankind, eat from whatever is on earth [that is] lawful (Halal) and good (Tayyib) and do not follow the footsteps of Shayṭan. Indeed, he is to you a clear enemy." (Quran 2:168)*

Importance of consuming lawful (Halal) and wholesome (Tayyib) foods

When discussing Islamic food rules, "halal" refers to what is considered acceptable or legal under Islamic law. The Quran, the sacred book of Islam, and the Hadith, the sayings and customs of Prophet Muhammad (PBUH), provide the rules for eating halal food. Beyond the kind of food eaten, the tenets of Halal also include the sources of components and how it is prepared.

The Importance of Halal Food

In Islam, halal food has great spiritual and cultural value. Eating halal food shows faith and submission to God's will, not just a way to satisfy nutritional requirements. Halal dietary regulations guide Muslims in choosing foods consistent with their religious views.

On the other hand, it includes all forms of movement allowed in Islam. Haram, occasionally referred to as non-Halal, is the antithesis of Halal. This is a reference to something that is forbidden by Islamic law. Even though it is frequently used for food, it can also be associated with other prohibited behaviours in Islam, such as corruption and theft, among many others.

Hazrat Saad (RA) relayed that The Prophet Muhammad (PBUH) said: "O Saad, purify your food (and as a result), you will become one whose supplications are accepted. I swear by He in whose hands the soul of Muhammad (PBUH) lies, verily a servant (of Allah SWT) tosses a Harām morsel in his stomach (due to which) no deed is accepted from him for 40 days." (Tabarani)

Principles of Halal Food:

The following are important halal food tenets:

- *Slaughtering (Zabiha):*

Slaughterer (Dhabiha): The individual carrying out the slaughter needs to be a Muslim who is of legal age and sound mind. This person is referred to as a "Dhabiha."

Invocation (Dhikr): At the moment of slaughter, the name of Allah (SWT) is called forth, acknowledging that the deed is being carried out for His benefit.

- *Haram and Halal Components:*

Alcohol and Intoxicants: Haram (forbidden) refers to any meal or beverage that contains alcohol or intoxicants.

Pork and its Byproducts: Goods that include pork or any byproducts are not considered Halal.

- *Outlawing Specific Animals:*

Pork and its Byproducts: Islam forbids the consumption of pork or any of its byproducts.

Predators and Carnivorous Animals: Predators are animals that are typically not eaten.

- *Blood and Related Substances:*

Blood Prohibition: Islam forbids the consumption of blood. Blood must be removed from meat using appropriate slaughter techniques.

In sum, Islamic dietary laws' halal principles extend beyond a food's permissibility. They include a range of moral and spiritual precepts that emphasise the significance of deliberate and conscientious consumption, encouraging a well-rounded way of living.

On the other hand, the Arabic words for pure and clean are the source of the name Tayyib. In a technical sense, it denotes a food's state of being devoid of all non-halal sources, hazardous substances, potential contamination, maintaining hygienic quality, and being safe to eat.

In another situation, the food does not achieve the Shariah-recommended level of good quality without tayyib components. This has inadvertently raised customer trust in the safety of food consumption. Organic food is one example of a food that satisfies the tayyib aspects since it is safer for consumers and devoid of chemical risks.

Muslims must be aware of and abide by the Islamic dietary regulations. Eating something that is forbidden by law displeases Allah (SWT) and may prevent one from making dua and being admitted into Paradise, as shown by the following hadith:

> *Abu Hurairah (RA) relayed that The Prophet Muhammad (PBUH) said: "O people! Allah is Pure and, therefore, accepts only that which is pure (Sahih Muslim)*

> *And He said: 'O you who believe (in the Oneness of Allah)! Eat of the lawful things that we have provided you...'" (Quran 2:172)*

> *The Prophet (PBUH) mentioned the person who travels for a long period of time; his hair is disheveled and covered with dust. He lifts his hand towards the sky and thus makes the supplication: 'My Rabb! My Rabb!' But his food is unlawful, his drink is unlawful, his clothes are unlawful, and his nourishment is unlawful; how can, then, his supplication be accepted?" (Sahih Muslim)*

Both bodily and spiritual health can be fulfilled by combining halal and tayyib components. This is since properly choosing halal and tayyib food is usually adequate to meet the body's nutritional needs while also potentially raising taqwa, or fear of Allah (SWT), and showing gratitude to Allah (SWT), who nourishes humans. Hence, Muslims must ensure that the food they eat satisfies the strict requirements of Halal and Tayyib, as demonstrated above.

Understanding the spiritual dimension of food and its impact on the soul

Food is more than just physical nourishment for the body; it has deep effects on the soul as well. Food's capacity to be more than just nourishment is demonstrated by its capacity to affect the soul. Food creates a tapestry of experiences that profoundly improve our lives, from attentive appreciation to emotional connections, cultural festivities, and culinary creativity.

Food nourishes not only our bodies but also our souls, tying us in incredibly meaningful ways to our history, present, and one another, whether we are gathered around a table with loved ones or discovering new flavours from far-off locations.

Eating with awareness encourages a link between our mental and physical well-being and serves as a reminder of life's small joys. By providing for the physical and spiritual needs of the body, this practice promotes a holistic approach to well-being. Food is a chance for mindfulness and presence in a world where life moves quickly. We develop a sense of thankfulness for the food we are given when we take the time to thoroughly enjoy every bite, recognising the complex flavours and textures.

Maintaining the physical body's health is crucial for the soul and spirit's well-being and our ability to achieve both material and spiritual goals. Eating halal food stresses the value of mental and spiritual cleanliness in addition to providing physical nourishment. Islam holds that the food we eat influences our spiritual health in addition to its physical effects.

We try to uphold purity in our thoughts, deeds, and character by avoiding haram (forbidden) meals and selecting halal options, which brings us closer to Allah (SWT). Even the most basic meal may deepen our spiritual connection to Allah (SWT) and improve our lives by choosing our food wisely and adjusting intentions towards Islamic values.

Eating Manners in Islam

Islam imposes strict rules and customs around eating that are seen to be necessary for preserving one's bodily and spiritual health. The following are some Islamic dining etiquette:

- Muslims say "Bismillah," which translates to "In the name of Allah," before eating.
- Muslims are advised to wash their hands before eating to maintain cleanliness and hygiene.
- Islam teaches its adherents to eat and drink with their right hand since it is more hygienic and deemed polite.
- Eating in moderation: In Islam, overindulging in food is frowned upon since it can impair physical health and breed spiritual sloth.

- Eating together: Islamic tradition encourages families and communities to eat together because it fosters a sense of fraternity and community.

- Eating from the closest side: Muslims are advised to eat from the side of the dish closest to them to prevent their hands from touching other people's plates.

- Expressing thankfulness to Allah after eating: Muslims say "Alhamdulillah," which translates to "All praise is due to Allah" after they have finished their meal.

Muslims think people can preserve good physical health and develop a sense of spirituality and gratitude towards Allah (SWT) by adhering to certain eating etiquette.

Practising Gratitude and Moderation in Eating Habits

In Islam, practising gratitude and moderation in eating habits is deeply intertwined with spiritual and physical well-being. These principles are encapsulated in various Islamic teachings that encourage mindful eating (Muraqabah) and avoiding wastefulness (Israf).

Mindful eating practices (Muraqabah) and avoiding wastefulness (Israf)

In Islam, mindful eating, or Muraqabah, involves being conscious and present during meals. This practice encourages Muslims to appreciate the food they consume, recognising it as a blessing from Allah. By being mindful, individuals can savour each bite, enhancing their gratitude for the sustenance provided.

The Prophet (PBUH) emphasised eating slowly, chewing thoroughly, and stopping before feeling overly full, which aligns with modern principles of healthy eating and mindfulness.

Avoiding wastefulness, or Israf, is a significant aspect of Islamic teachings. The Quran explicitly advises against wasting resources, including food.

> *Allah says, "Eat and drink but be not excessive. Indeed, He likes not those who commit excess." (Quran 7:31)*

By taking only what is necessary and ensuring that no food is wasted, Muslims show respect and gratitude for the blessings they receive.

This principle not only promotes personal health but also aligns with broader goals of sustainability and environmental stewardship.

Adopting a balanced diet (Mizan) for physical and spiritual well-being

A balanced diet is defined as one that includes a range of foods and sufficient quantities of the nutrients required for optimal health. Maintaining a healthy and fit body requires a balanced diet.

The divine directive to eat the permissible foods that Allah (SWT) has created for humans is found in the Holy Quran. Islam advises us to adopt a balanced diet since it can keep us healthy – the Holy Quran advocates a balanced diet and eating in moderation.

> *Allah (SWT) stated: "And He enforced the balance. That you exceed not the bounds; but observe the balance strictly, and fall not short thereof." (Quran 55:7-9)*

About overindulgence and food waste, our beloved Prophet Muhammad (PBUH) said in one of his hadiths:

> *"No human being has ever filled a container worse than his own stomach. The son of Adam needs no more than a few morsels of food to keep up his strength; doing so, he should consider that a third of his stomach is for food, a third for drink and a third for breathing." (Ibn Majah)*

The following list of nutritious meals that the Holy Prophet (PBUH) enjoyed eating is also the best:

- *Honey*

In the morning, the Prophet (PBUH) would sip water and honey. Honey is the drink of drinks, the food of foods, and the drug of medications. It can be used as a mouthwash, hair conditioner, eye soother, and meat preservative, as well as to strengthen the stomach and get rid of phlegm.

> *The Prophet (PBUH) said, "Honey is the cure for every stomach disease" (Sahih Bukhari)*

- *Dates*

The Prophet (PBUH) cherished eating dates. Dates are low in fat since they do not contain cholesterol, a good source of calcium, potassium, dietary fibre, vitamin B6, and vitamin A.

- *Milk*

Milk contains calcium for teeth and bones, strengthens the back, restores vision, and enhances memory.

- *Vinegar*

Vinegar is nutritious and aids in the recovery of weary muscles following strenuous exercise.

- *Figs*

Figs are healthy for your bones and low in calories. They provide a range of nutrients, antioxidants, and health advantages and are also referred to as one of the fruits of paradise.

> *"By the fig and the olive, And [by] Mount Sinai, And [by] this secure city [Makkah], We have certainly created man in the best of stature." (Quran, 95:1-4)*

- *Olives*

Olives are also mentioned in the Holy Quran. Olive oil is a fantastic skin and hair treatment, curing stomach inflammation and postponing ageing.

> *Prophet Muhammad (PBUH) said: "Eat the olive oil and apply it (locally), since there is a cure for seventy diseases in it, one of them is Leprosy." (Ibn Majah)*

- *Grapes*

Grapes were a favourite food of the Prophet (PBUH). Because of their high fibre content, they help to strengthen the kidneys, clean the intestines, and purify the blood.

The Quran and the Holy Prophet's (PBUH) Sunnah provide insight into the significance of eating a healthy, balanced diet. Islam has always strongly emphasised the value of a healthy, balanced diet.

Foods included in the Holy Quran are essential to a healthy lifestyle and a good source of nutrition. As Muslims, we ought to follow these suggested guidelines for a healthy diet and urge our children to do the same.

Advice for Mindful and Healthful Eating

Although it may seem paradoxical to approach eating with an emphasis on mindfulness and health, this is actually possible, particularly when one remembers that Islam promotes healthy eating while appreciating the blessings Allah (SWT) has bestowed upon us.

Eating with awareness involves considering what you eat, taking your time, not being sidetracked, and relishing every taste. Maintaining a balanced diet is advised for your health, and you should enjoy culinary treats because nothing should be done carelessly or in excess.

Engaging in physical exercise after adhering to a well-crafted eating plan that promotes health and mindfulness is crucial to sustaining optimal fitness. Physical activity can enhance cardiovascular health, increase muscle mass, and burn calories. Muslims can engage in a variety of halal physical activities, including biking, hiking, swimming, walking, jogging, and yoga. Various exercise positions included in the Salah prayer also aid in burning calories and maintaining an active physique throughout the day.

In sum, Islamic teachings on gratitude and moderation in eating emphasise mindful eating, avoiding wastefulness, and adopting a balanced diet. These practices foster a deeper appreciation for food as a divine blessing, promote physical health, and support spiritual growth, thereby leading to a harmonious and fulfilling life in accordance with Islamic principles.

Chapter Seven

Self-Care and Well-Being

Anything you do to maintain your physical, mental, emotional, social, and spiritual well-being is considered self-care. If you do not take regular time for self-care, you risk being burned out and endangering your health. Making time for self-care is something that many individuals find difficult.

A common misperception is that taking care of oneself is selfish, although this could not be further from the reality. Taking care of oneself is essential to taking care of others. Taking care of yourself can make you feel good, which increases motivation and self-worth and gives you more energy to assist your loved ones and yourself.

The key to self-care is finding balance and listening to your body and mind when they tell you it is time. The primary purpose of self-care is to live a happier and healthier life.

Islam clarifies that Allah (SWT) values each human being as unique and distinct. That is why Islam teaches us the value of self-care, emphasising it as a way to express gratitude to Allah (SWT) for the priceless gift of health and fitness, increasing productivity and leading a happier life. Therefore, how can Muslims who practise self-care position themselves for holistic success in this life as well as the next?

The key is to apply the teachings of the Quran and the Prophet's (PBUH) Sunnah to incorporate small self-care practices into our everyday routines. Let's delve into it!

Prophetic Guidance on Self-Care and Hygiene

Islam strongly emphasises maintaining one's physical and spiritual purity and self-care. Islam teaches that looking after oneself is a spiritual as well as a bodily necessity. It defines self-care as a wide range of practices, including attending to one's mental, emotional, and physical well-being.

For example, maintaining personal hygiene, cleanliness, and a healthy lifestyle are recommended in Islam. Muslims are also urged to take care of their mental health by practising stress-relieving hobbies like exercise and meditation.

Furthermore, Islam promotes taking care of one's body by eating a balanced diet, getting adequate sleep, exercising regularly, and seeking medical attention when necessary. The Prophet Muhammad (PBUH) himself urged his followers to prioritise their health and well-being and stressed the value of doing so.

All things considered, Islamic teachings place a high value on self-care and view it as a way to achieve a healthy balance between life's spiritual and physical realms.

Our everyday routine shows that we frequently disregard our health in a variety of ways. Most people do not adhere to a schedule, which ultimately results in a hectic and disorganised way of life. If we wake early and stay up late, particularly on the weekends, miss or postpone meals, delay pray, and mishandle or ignore household tasks, our health will undoubtedly suffer. We should remember that self-care is a form of ibadah.

The mind, soul, and body are the three fundamental components of human beings. The human body depends on the other two and is made up of and connected to them. Without also taking care of the mind and the soul, taking care of the body would not be complete.

Though it may appear self-serving, taking care of oneself is not selfish in the slightest. We are entwined with numerous other lives. Allah (SWT) made humans so that social interaction is a given. You can take care of your loved ones and society as a whole if you are sound and healthy. So, always prioritise self-care. It is necessary for overall well-being.

Types of Self-Care

Self-care can take up any form, a few specific of them mentioned below:

- **Physical**

Islam advises Muslims to take good care of their physical well-being by following a nutritious diet, regular exercise, and proper hygiene. Overindulgence in unhealthy food might result in health issues. Prophet Muhammad (PBUH) encouraged his people to eat in moderation and to maintain a healthy weight.

Maintain a healthy diet:

Islam also places a high value on nutrition, and the Prophet Muhammad's (PBUH) Sunnah offers comprehensive instructions for maintaining a well-balanced diet. The Prophet (PBUH) exhorts Muslims to eat various foods that provide their bodies with all the necessary nutrients.

His choice of basic, as opposed to opulent, meals, established an example for others.

Hazrat Aisyah (RA) has said: "The Messenger of God never complained about simple food." (Sahih Muslim)

Chewing food properly is another crucial component of having a nutritious diet, according to the Sunnah. We are taught by the Prophet (PBUH) to thoroughly chew our meal before swallowing.

Prophet Muhammad (PBUH) said: "When one of you eats, he should chew his food thoroughly." (Abu Daud)

Islam places a high value on fasting, which is also very beneficial to health. Fasting aids in weight loss, immune system stimulation, metabolism rise, and toxin removal from the body.

Hence, we can preserve our physical and mental well-being by eating a balanced and modest diet. According to the Sunnah, eating healthily benefits individuals and is a deed that pleases Allah (SWT). As a means of worship and health maintenance, let us follow the Sunnah and adopt a healthy eating lifestyle.

Physical Exercise:

In Islam, maintaining physical health goes beyond the surface goal of having a flawless body; it involves taking care of one's body and soul. Muslims can complete their religious duties, improve their spiritual health, and live an Islamically-guided life by staying physically healthy.

Rest and Sleep:

Adequate rest and sleep are essential for physical and mental health. The Quran mentions the importance of sleep as a means of rest:

"And We made your sleep [a means for] rest." (Quran 78:9)

The Prophet Muhammad (PBUH) advised his followers to balance their time between worship, work, and rest:

> *"Your body has a right over you, your eyes have a right over you, and your wife has a right over you." (Sahih Bukhari)*

Cleanliness and Personal Hygiene:

Islam places great emphasis on cleanliness and personal hygiene.

> *Prophet Muhammad (PBUH) said: "Cleanliness is half of faith." (Sahih Muslim)*

In conclusion, physical self-care is deeply rooted in Islamic teachings. These practices not only contribute to physical well-being but also to spiritual and mental health, aligning with the holistic approach of Islam to human health and well-being.

- **Spiritual Self-Care**

Islam emphasises the need for spiritual self-care to develop a closer relationship with Allah (SWT) and find inner serenity. As Muslims, we recognise the significance of maintaining a close relationship with Allah (SWT).

It is about building a relationship with our Creator that can significantly influence our lives, not merely about following rituals. It takes intentional measures to develop our faith and establish a deep connection with Allah (SWT).

Frequent prayer and Quran recitation serve as reminders of our life's purpose and the ideals and standards we ought to pursue. Through these acts of worship, we can speak with Allah (SWT) and ask for His blessings and guidance.

We can also fortify our relationship with Him by performing deeds of love and generosity. Not only does helping the less fortunate benefit them, but it also purifies our spirits, strengthens our faith, and increases our humility.

Establishing a relationship with Allah (SWT) is an individual path that necessitates us taking ownership of maintaining our religion. By dedicating our lives to Allah (SWT) and His teachings, we may lead meaningful lives, inspire and mentor people around us, and realise our own desires. We must work to deepen our relationship with Him and reap the benefits it can bring about in our lives.

- **Mental Self-Care**

Self-care is crucial to improving mental health in the Islamic setting because it fosters inner refuge and self-compassion. This action reminds us that taking care of oneself is crucial to our general well-being, which aligns with Islamic beliefs.

Islam advises Muslims to take care of their minds by abstaining from stress, anger, and bad ideas because it acknowledges the significance of mental health. Maintaining mental well-being can be effectively achieved by mindfulness, meditation, and information seeking, as taught by the Quran and Hadith.

Maintaining a positive mindset and being grateful for Allah's (SWT) blessings can improve mental health. The Quran emphasises gratitude:

> "And [remember] when your Lord proclaimed, 'If you are grateful, I will surely increase you [in favour]; but if you deny, indeed, my punishment is severe." (Quran 14:7)

The Prophet Muhammad (PBUH) said:

> "*Amazing is the affair of the believer, verily his entire affair is good and this is not for no one except the believer. If something of good/happiness befalls him, he is grateful, and that is good for him. If something of harm befalls him, he is patient, and that is good for him.*"
> *(Sahih Muslim)*

In Islam, self-care is a holistic practice encompassing physical, spiritual, and mental well-being. Each aspect is intertwined, promoting a balanced and harmonious life that aligns with Islamic teachings.

- **Other considerations of self-care**

Practise self-love: Realising that loving oneself is not selfish is crucial. It is a crucial component of self-care, which is both required and beneficial. One definition of self-love is being kind to oneself. Since both self-care and self-love refer to the activities we do for ourselves, they are comparable. However, self-love centres on loving and caring for oneself, whereas self-care refers to your actions to take care of yourself. You have to prioritise your needs when it comes to self-love and self-care.

Take self-care as 'acts of kindness': Consider the steps you take to take care of yourself as "acts of kindness" in the same way that you might regard the steps you take to take care of others, especially if you battle with guilt or are very hard on yourself. If you find yourself worrying or torn about whether to put yourself first, you might discover that it helps to set your intention. Before starting a self-care activity, you may set an intention like this: "I am going to finish this to feel happy and stress-free."

Practise gratitude: Gratitude can have a profoundly beneficial impact on our sense of wellness. Recalling the positive aspects of life can be a straightforward yet effective self-care practice. It can assist us in adopting a more upbeat outlook and directing our attention towards more encouraging things. An essential component of Islamic faith and culture is the practice of thankfulness.

Practising self-love, viewing self-care as acts of kindness, and practising gratitude are essential for balanced well-being, fostering a positive outlook, and aligning with Islamic teachings. Prioritising these aspects helps individuals lead a harmonious and fulfilling life.

The Importance of Purification in Islam

In Islamic jurisprudence, the term "taharah" denotes cleanliness or purity. Taharah is crucial to maintaining both bodily and spiritual cleanliness in Islamic tradition. It must be done before engaging in certain acts of worship, such as saying the Quran aloud and praying.

Islam views prayers as a kind of worship that necessitates a state of cleanliness and purity, which is why taharah is so important. Muslims, depending on their degree of ritual impurity, must perform wudu or ghusl prior to prayer. For mild impurities, wudu is done; for major pollutants, ghusl is needed.

Even if someone prays without the required Taharah, the prayer is still seen as legitimate and full. Taharah is, therefore, necessary for Muslims to perform acts of worship such as prayer. Because of this significance, taharah is full of virtues.

Taharah, or cleanliness and purification, is highly valued in Islam since it is seen as a cornerstone of the faith. Quran and the Sunnah of the Prophet (PBUH) describe the merits of taharah as follows:

> *"Truly, Allah loves those who turn to Him constantly, and He loves those who keep themselves pure and clean."*
> *(Quran 2:222)*

> *The Holy Prophet (PBUH) said: "the key to paradise is prayer, and the key to prayer is cleanliness." (Ibn Majah)*

In the pursuit of pleasing Al Quddus, the Most Pure Allah (SWT), we Muslims aim for two kinds of cleanliness.

Primary purification, or Taharah al-kubra, is necessary following a condition of ritual impurity, which includes ejaculation, menstruation, postpartum haemorrhage, and sexual activity. It entails giving yourself a thorough body wash with water during a ghusl or complete bath or shower.

Minor purification, or Taharah al-sughra, is necessary for doing daily tasks like handling the Quran and praying. It entails the wudu, or washing of certain body parts, such as the hands, nostrils, mouth, face, arms, head, and feet.

Benefits of Taharah

Islam's central idea of taharah emphasises the need to maintain bodily and spiritual purity. It is not just about keeping the body clean; it is also about keeping the soul pure. Muslims can stay physically healthy and stop the spread of disease by keeping their bodies clean through bathing and ablution. By upholding both physical and spiritual cleanliness, Muslims can live a healthy, moral, and Allah-pleasing life.

Islam teaches that purifying oneself, or taharah, before participating in any kind of devotion, including prayer, represents humility and surrender to Allah (SWT). Through this act of purification, the believer is reminded of their dependency on Allah (SWT) and humble position before Him.

Islam requires taharah, or purity, as a requirement before engaging in any act of worship, such as the hajj or prayer. This highlights how crucial it is to approach Allah (SWT) in a clean physical and spiritual state. Physical preparation entails cleansing oneself by ablution (wudu) or washing (ghusl).

It also strengthens the believer's bond with Allah (SWT), showing that they are prepared to obey Him and follow in His footsteps. The believer seeks cleansing and accepts their impurities through this act of Taharah, which enhances their spiritual state and fortifies their relationship with Allah (SWT).

Avoiding sins, confessing one's faults, and purifying one's intents are all part of spiritual preparation. Thanks to this preparation, the believer can approach worship with a pure heart and mind, free from interruptions and impurities. As a result, taharah is crucial to the practice of Islam since it enables the believer to connect with Allah (SWT) and perform acts of worship while being pious and dedicated.

Taharah in Islam strongly emphasises cleanliness and personal hygiene, essential for living a wholesome and balanced life. Maintaining physical health and halting the transmission of disease can be accomplished with good hygiene and cleanliness.

In addition to physically cleaning oneself, ablution or ghusl, which are Islamic purifying rites, also foster a sense of cleanliness and well-being. This can stop the spread of disease and encourage good health, both of which are necessary for a healthy society. Taharah is, therefore, an essential custom that supports cleanliness, personal hygiene, and general well-being.

Taharah, which emphasises both spiritual and physical purity, serves as a reminder to Muslims of the highest level of purification needed for the Hereafter. Muslims believe that on the Day of Judgement, they shall be perfectly clean and pure before Allah (SWT).

Taharah reminds us of the significance of living a pure and upright life and prepares us for the last purification. It cultivates good manners and etiquette while benefiting the individual in this life as well as the next. It also fosters community cohesion and respect for others.

Prioritising Mental Health and Emotional Balance

Seeking support (Nasiha) and counselling in times of distress

Islam advises believers to talk things over and get guidance from one another to learn other people's perspectives. Both the person and society benefit from this. It fosters intelligence and increases self-worth. It fortifies ties between individuals and fosters harmony and togetherness within the community.

We occasionally find ourselves in difficult situations and require Islamic guidance. Islam is based on the genuine understanding of Allah's (SWT) teachings and those of His Messenger (PBUH). As a result, the Quran and Sunnah provide Muslims with all the guidance they need to maintain their faith.

Therefore, we are urged to consult experts. But getting Islamic counsel involves more than merely reading dubious online articles or asking any Muslim you come across a question about. To avoid being duped, Muslims like us should be careful about where we get our Islamic guidance.

Muslims have access to a wealth of information, yet if we look for answers on our own, we still face the risk of being misled. For Islamic advice, consult your local imams or someone who has demonstrated knowledge of the subject you are asking for assistance on. Even though your uncle has been married for forty years, this does not imply that he understands marital fiqh. Asking someone who is most likely winging it themselves is not wise. You need a guide who will lead you in accordance with the Sunnah and the Quran.

"And cooperate in righteousness and piety, but do not cooperate in sin and aggression. And fear Allah; indeed, Allah is severe in penalty." (Quran 5:2)

"Religion is sincere advice." We said, "To whom?" He said, "To Allah, His Book, His Messenger, and to the leaders of the Muslims and their common folk." (Sahih Muslim)

In Islam, seeking support and counselling during times of distress is essential for maintaining mental and emotional balance. Turning to trusted individuals for Nasiha can provide valuable insights and emotional comfort, aligning with the communal and supportive nature of Islamic teachings.

Incorporating stress management strategies

In today's fast-paced world, many people struggle to manage their stress. No matter one's religion or cultural upbringing, the rigours of contemporary life can be overwhelming. However, Muslims have access to a wealth of practical stress-reduction strategies and spiritual instruction. Let's examine stress-reduction techniques that will help you feel less stressed and live a better overall life.

Salah's calming rhythm: Salah, or regular prayers, helps us stay constantly aligned with our life's purpose. Specifically, the act of prostration represents letting go and putting one's reliance on Allah (SWT). This small gesture can frequently provide a great deal of relief.

Through Quran and Sunnah: Numerous lessons on self-care are provided by the Quran and Sunnah, which can aid in stress management. The Prophet (PBUH), for instance, stressed the value of getting adequate sleep, maintaining a healthy diet, and setting aside time for leisure and relaxation. Making self-care a priority and abiding by the Sunnah will help you feel less stressed and enhance your general health and wellness.

Shukr (gratitude) and optimistic thinking: Gratitude practice, or Shukr, is another powerful stress-reduction technique. By emphasising the good things in your life and showing thankfulness for what you have, you can change your perspective to one that is more optimistic. This can help you maintain resilience and motivation in the face of stress and hardship.

Good social networks and assistance: Having supportive and positive social networks can also be beneficial for stress management. Surrounding yourself with encouraging and cheerful people can make you feel more rooted and connected. Furthermore, asking for assistance and support from others when required may be a very helpful strategy for stress management and conquering obstacles.

Breathing methods and unwinding: Stress management strategies might also benefit from breathing exercises and relaxation techniques. These techniques may ease your mind, relax your body, and slow your breathing. By incorporating these skills into your regular practice, you may manage stressful situations with composure and awareness.

Acceptance: Last but not least, having faith in Allah (SWT) and yielding to His will might be effective strategies for stress reduction. By accepting that everything occurs for a reason and having faith in Allah's (SWT) plan, you can develop inner serenity and resilience. Furthermore, focusing on the things you can control and letting go of worry and anxiety are two benefits of accepting the things that are out of your control.

Stress is a natural part of life. We get relief and strengthen our spiritual base by accepting the. By implementing these practices, we can lower our stress levels and enhance our general quality of life.

Chapter Eight

Mindfulness in Prayer and Salah

Enhancing Khushu (Concentration) in Salah

One of the heart's actions is khushu, which means to sink, be low, be obedient, and be still. In technical terms, it describes the heart's total devotion to Allah (SWT). Khushu is a spirit that lives in the heart and expresses itself through the organs and limbs.

When you experience khushu, your heart softens, stills, and humbles itself before its Lord. Your heart becomes so devoted to Allah (SWT) and submits to Him that everything else becomes insignificant. Your organs and limbs are then humbled, following the heart's lead.

> *The Prophet of Allah (PBUH) said, "There is a lump of flesh in the body: if it is sound, the whole body will be sound, but if it is corrupt, the whole body will be corrupt. Truly, it is the heart." (Sahih Bukhari)*

Khushu lights your heart with the "light" of Allah's (SWT) magnificence and puts out the "fires" of want and desire. Your heart is filled with Allah's (SWT) adoration when you fully realise He is staring at you.

Khushu in salah is the practice of praying calmly and deliberately when bowing and prostrating, between the two prostrations, and upon rising again. It entails humility and total mental focus.

The essence of prayer is to focus on and remain humble in prayer. This is one of the most crucial things to do. Consequently, we must be mindful of centring the prayer with appropriate humility and completing it calmly and deliberately when we prostrate and bow, between the two prostrations and when we stand up again after bowing.

> *In the Quran, Allah says: "Indeed, the believers, who have Khushu' in their Salah, are the winners." (Quran 23:1-2)*

The worshipper's prayer is invalid if he is too fast, fails to concentrate and exhibits humility to the point where it seems like he is pecking his way through the prayer. However, if he is relaxed and prays slowly, his thoughts occasionally stray, or he forgets; this does not make his prayer ineffective.

Rather, his prayer will only be rewarded insofar as it was directed, and he demonstrated appropriate humility and awareness of Allah (SWT); he will be rewarded for that, but he will not be rewarded for the portions of his prayer in which he was not focused. Thus, he needs to slowly concentrate on his prayer and offer it, demonstrating humility before Allah (SWT).

Khushu rewards virtuous deeds with multiplicity and magnificence. Although reciting Surah al-Ikhlaṣ (equivalent to one-third of the Quran) has a significant reward, Ibn Taymiyyah (RA) explains that reading any other ayah with khushu would have a bigger benefit.

Moreover, it is crucial to remember that you ought to try to attain khushu inside and outside of ṣalah. According to Imam al-Ghazali (RA), khushu is the outcome of Iman and a strong belief in Allah's

(SWT) majesty. If this comes your way, you will experience khushu both within and outside of ṣalah, even while you are alone.

A perpetual state of khushu can be attained by always recalling that Allah (SWT) observes you, marvelling at His majesty, and acknowledging your shortcomings. When you are in a condition of khushu (SWT), you are overcome with humility and a deep need for Allah (SWT) because you continuously weigh your sins against His magnificence. The path is complex. The process of growing closer to experiencing such beauty and serenity in our salah is what counts. Let's see how to do it effectively.

Techniques for improving focus and presence during prayers

As you pray, you are trying to focus, but now and then, something else distracts you. Are you unable to recall the verses that just passed by your lips? It takes a lot of devotion to control your focus during prayer. We will talk about some techniques for focusing during prayer now.

Understanding Allah (SWT)'s Presence

Always keep in mind that God is aware of all you do. A Muslim is known for his taqwa, or awareness of God, which inspires him to do good deeds and keeps him from committing sins. It is a quality that will benefit you in your daily life as well as when you pray—keeping God before you is the finest posture for prayer. Death is something that is behind you, and that can happen to you at any time. Heaven is on your right side with all its splendour and delights. Hell, with its fire and penalties, is to your left.

Consider and comprehend the words you are reciting.

Knowing enough Arabic to comprehend what you are saying in prayer increases your awareness during prayer and allows the words of the Quran to enter your heart. This is another part of being able to understand the Quran. Additionally, carrying what you will recite while deliberately choosing what to say can help you become more focused and attentive during prayer.

Be sure to eliminate anything that may impair your ability to focus during prayer.

Determine what in your environment is causing the most problems. After determining the sources, compile a list and devise a plan of attack. It is not our intention to imply that you will be able to eliminate every possible distraction. It is not feasible, and you should not anticipate it.

Try to reduce the things that make you less focused when you pray. If you cannot concentrate, the next step is to travel to a peaceful location. One of the best methods to ignore disruptions is to alter the atmosphere. A new environment revitalises your sensations, improving your focus.

Recite slowly.

You ought to make an effort to pray slowly. Why are you rushing, and what is the purpose? Our main goal in life is to worship, and this class revolves around the Salah. Let us attempt to pronounce the verses slowly, pausing briefly in between each one as we pray.

Plan your day while remembering to pray.

Nothing worthwhile comes easily; we must exert much effort to succeed. This also applies to prayerful concentrations. If you find it difficult to focus during prayers, it is advisable to plan your day. Your mind is racing with everything you need to get done. Keep a journal of your daily activities and set out a specified time each day for prayer to help you focus better when you pray. A prudent individual always plans their movements to maximise their time. Organise yourself and proceed with a specific goal in mind. Making a schedule for your day will help you focus better and reduce mental strain.

Improving your salah is a lifetime journey. These practices must be applied daily. There will be times when we lose focus and revert to unhealthy behaviours. Keep trying and never give up. Insha'Allah, with consistent practice, our salah will get better with time.

Ask Allah Almighty to assist you in getting there. Allah (SWT) is delighted when His servants attempt to approach Him. If we take ten steps toward Him, He will run 100 steps to reach us.

Overcoming distractions and maintaining spiritual connection

The world is rife with diversions. Distraction is being conditioned in our brains. Text messages, push notifications, advertisements, Instagram posts, emails, and the list goes on and on, interrupting our days nonstop. If we are not careful with this enhanced connectivity, we risk losing touch with Allah Almighty (SWT), our Creator.

"Anything that diverts your attention from something you want to concentrate on" is a basic definition of distraction. Shaytan's goal for us is precisely this. Shaytan adores Muslims who are easily sidetracked. It does not matter to him what that item is. He merely wishes to divert our focus from Allah's affairs.

Naturally, Shaytan tries to take all actions possible to ensure that we do not first accept Allah (SWT) as our Lord and Saviour. The best thing he can do after losing that battle, though, is to ensure that Muslims become as distracted as possible. In a society where distractions abound, we can maintain our spiritual attention in these ways:

- Daily Prayers (Salah): Perform the five daily prayers on time with devotion.

- Quran Recitation: Regularly read and reflect on the meanings of the Qur'an.

- Supplication (Dua): Engage in heartfelt supplications, expressing needs and gratitude.

- Remembrance (Dhikr): Recite phrases like "SubhanAllah," "Alhamdulillah," and "Allahu Akbar."

- Seeking Knowledge: Learn more about Islam through lectures and books.

- Charity (Sadaqah): Perform acts of charity and kindness to purify the heart.

- Fasting: Observe both obligatory and voluntary fasts to enhance spirituality.

Maintaining a strong spiritual connection with Allah (SWT) is essential to a Muslim's life. These practices collectively foster a deeper and more meaningful connection with Him.

Understanding the Spiritual Dimensions of Salah

Exploring the inner dimensions (Batin) of ritual worship (Zahir)

The term "salah" in Arabic refers to the five times a day Muslims are required to offer the ritual prayer. It is one of Islam's five pillars. An essential component of a Muslim's life is salah. Muslims are obligated to reflect on the words of the Quran, the Shahadah (the profession of faith), and the qualities of Allah (SWT) during their daily prayers. Muslims from all over the world gather for worship at five designated times every day, facing the Kaaba in Mecca, as a way to connect with Allah (SWT) and their life's purpose—to remember and worship Him.

Allah says in the Quran: "Maintain with care the (obligatory) prayers and (in particular) the middle prayer and stand before Allah, devoutly obedient." (Quran 2:238)

In addition to the five required prayers (Fajr, Dhuhr, Asr, Maghrib, Isha), Muslims are also permitted to offer Sunnah and Nafl Salah. The Prophet (PBUH) regularly gave the Sunnah Salah (prayers) as voluntary worship at predetermined times and locations. At any moment throughout the day, Muslims can offer Nafl Salah as an additional form of Ibadah (worship).

> *The Prophet Muhammad (PBUH) said: "Between a man and disbelief or polytheism is the abandonment of Salah." (Sahih Muslim)*

While the outward form, or Zahir, of Salah is crucial, its true depth and transformative power lie in its inner dimensions, known as Batin. This inner aspect involves the worshiper's spiritual and emotional engagement to create a profound connection with Allah (SWT).

The Outward Form (Zahir) of Salah

The physical components of Salah include:

- Takbir: The opening declaration of "Allahu Akbar" (God is the Greatest).
- Qiyam: Standing and reciting verses from the Quran.
- Ruku: Bowing with hands on knees.
- Sujud: Prostrating with forehead, nose, hands, knees, and toes touching the ground.
- Tashahhud: Sitting and reciting specific prayers.
- Taslim: Concluding the prayer with salutations of peace.

These actions are performed with precise movements and recitations, embodying the discipline and structure of Islamic worship.

The Inner Dimensions (Batin) of Salah

The inner dimensions of Salah focus on the spiritual and emotional states that should accompany the physical actions. These include:

Sincerity (Ikhlas)

- Performing Salah solely for the sake of Allah (SWT), free from any desire for recognition or praise from others.
- Ensuring that the intention (Niyyah) behind each prayer is pure and directed towards seeking closeness to Allah (SWT).

Humility (Khushu)

- Cultivating a sense of awe and reverence towards Allah (SWT).
- Acknowledging one's dependence on Allah (SWT) and submitting fully to His will.

Reflection (Tafakkur)

- Meditating on the greatness of Allah (SWT) and His creation.
- Using the moments of stillness in Salah to contemplate one's relationship with Allah (SWT) and the purpose of life.

Love and Longing (Mahabbah wa Shawq)

- Developing a deep love for Allah (SWT) and a yearning to draw closer to Him.
- Feeling joy and contentment in performing Salah as an expression of love and devotion.

The true essence of Salah is realised when the outward actions (Zahir) are harmonised with the inner spiritual states (Batin). This integration transforms Salah from a mere ritual to a profound spiritual experience.

Chapter Nine

Practising Patience and Gratitude

Virtues of Sabr (Patience) and Shukr (Gratitude)

The globe is coming together to confront something never seen before. For months to come, thousands will continue to feel the problems, hardships, and difficulties it has brought. We trust that we will all learn from this experience and begin to appreciate life's small pleasures once more.

Thanks to Allah (SWT), Islam has given us direction and insight into a wide range of circumstances, including difficult ones. Allah (SWT) and the Prophet (PBUH) have given us two distinct strategies that we can apply based on the situation: patience (Sabr) and gratitude (Shukr).

What is Sabr?

Translations of the Arabic word "sabr" commonly render it as "patience," "perseverance," or "steadfastness". Just as the head is essential to the body, so is patience (sabr) to faith (iman). Without the head, the body ceases to exist; similarly, without patience, faith disappears. The patient is described as follows in the Quran:

> *"And give good news to the patient – those who, when an affliction visits them, say, 'Indeed we belong to Allah, and to Him do we indeed return'." (Quran 2:155-156)*

It is bearing with and surviving adversity without losing our poise and serenity. Whether handling a difficult assignment at work or a personal catastrophe, sabr can support us in being resilient and powerful.

> *Allah says in the Quran: "Indeed Allah is with the patient." (Quran 2:153)*

Every believer will certainly experience many hardships, challenges, and difficulties during their lifetime. These trials occasionally involve him, occasionally involve his fortune, and occasionally include his loved ones.

The believer will be touched by these predetermined trials and calamities from the All-Wise One in many ways; if he has the wrong perspective on the testing subject, he may make grave mistakes, especially because some of the disasters are severe and unbearable.

Many individuals are unaware of the lessons that can be learned from trials and testing; they might not realise that Allah (SWT) tests us out of mercy rather than retribution. To have a solid understanding of the subject of ibtilaa' (tests and trials), a believer should examine it through the lens of the Quranic textual proofs and the genuine Sunnah of the Prophet (PBUH).

The believer seeks recompense through adversity, and the only way to achieve this is with patience, which can only be shown via strong resolve and unwavering faith.

> *And Allah tells us: And We will surely test you with something of fear and hunger and a loss of wealth and lives and fruits, but give good tidings to the patient, Who, when a museebah (calamity) strikes them, say, "Indeed we belong to Allah, and indeed to Him we will return." Those are the ones upon whom are blessings from their Lord and mercy. And it is those who are the [rightly] guided. (Quran 2:155-57)*

> *Moreover, the Prophet tells us that True patience is at the first stroke of calamity. (Sahih Bukhari)*

The hadith and this verse stress how crucial patience is when facing adversity. What does it mean to remain patient in the face of such extreme hardship or at "the first stroke of calamity"? From where does patience originate?

Genuine patience comes from the heart and is strongly correlated with our level of relationship with Allah (SWT). When our souls are connected to Him, we completely acknowledge that Allah (SWT) is in total control of our lives. It becomes easier to be patient when faced with difficulties.

There will always be hardships in life, and ideal circumstances may never come. In actuality, things may even become harder. The key questions to ask yourself are: What is your mission, and what value are you offering? Remember, even when it does not feel like it, practising Sabr (patience) will always lead to improvement. If you are not growing, you are stagnating.

What is Shukr?

Shukr is the Arabic term for thankfulness or expressing thankfulness. The idea of appreciation is very significant in Islam. Being appreciative and expressing thankfulness to Allah (SWT) is a kind of worship; on the other hand, being unthankful indicates one's lack of confidence in Allah (SWT).

Similar to patience, most of us have a theoretical understanding of gratitude. We understand how important it is to acknowledge the blessings in our lives. As an idea, we understand it. And for many of us, gratitude for life's blessings comes quite naturally. This is emphasised in numerous verses of the Quran.

> *Allah tells us: Then remember Me; I will remember you.*
> *Be grateful to Me, and do not reject Me. (Quran 2:152)*

Many of us identify being patient during difficult times and grateful during happy ones. But gratitude is frequently necessary if we are to patiently overcome a problem in life. And we need patience to be genuinely grateful for a blessing. A closer examination reveals the significant connection between appreciation and patience.

Thus, for Iman to be fulfilled, patience and gratitude are required. These days, there are many stories of people favoured with numerous gifts from Allah (SWT), yet they live in such a rush that they hardly ever take the time to express gratitude to Allah (SWT) or remember that He is the source of all their blessings. They miss the "signs" of Allah (SWT) in the mercies all around them because they are impatient enough to express their thankfulness.

In the face of adversity, we also witness individuals who cannot recognise any positive aspects of their situation. They cannot recognise the "signs" of what is occurring to them because they lack the gratitude that would enable them to exercise patience. It is possible that practising patience in both difficult and easy situations, as well as gratitude in both situations when faced with difficulties and blessings, is what our Iman needs to be totally complete.

Developing resilience (Sumud) in facing life's challenges

Gaining resilience, or the capacity to adjust and bounce back from setbacks and hardships, is an essential life skill for everyone. Islam offers a distinctive viewpoint on resilience, highlighting the significance of patience, persistence, and faith in Allah (SWT) in overcoming life's obstacles. If we do not learn to be patient and resilient, we risk becoming overwhelmed in trying circumstances, which can worsen stress, anxiety, depression, and other mental health conditions.

Resilience and patience enable us to deal with hardship constructively. When faced with adversity, patience enables us to remain composed and hold fast to our beliefs. Resilience provides us with the ability to overcome obstacles and move forward. When combined, they keep us from giving up or sinking into despair.

Resilience and patience also allow us to help those facing comparable difficulties. Being compassionate travellers on other people's journeys is made possible by the understanding of empathy we acquire from our own struggles. Family members, friends, and neighbours enduring life's challenges might draw inspiration from our tenacity.

> *The Quran states, "And seek help through patience and prayer, and indeed, it is difficult except for the humbly submissive [to Allah]." (Quran 2:45)*

This verse highlights the value of prayer and patience when asking for assistance when things are tough. Muslims are urged to seek Allah's assistance and direction in overcoming life's obstacles. The Prophet (PBUH) is a prime example of tenacity in Islam. Throughout his life, he had many difficulties and setbacks, yet he never wavered in his commitment to his purpose and religion.

> *The Messenger of Allah (PBUH) said, "Strange are the ways of a believer, for there is good in every affair of his, and this is not the case with anyone else except in the case of a believer: if he has an occasion to feel delight, he thanks (God), thus there is a good for him in it, and if he gets into trouble and shows resignation (and endures it patiently), there is a good for him in it". (Sahih Muslim)*

This hadith highlights the need for resilience in Islam and the ability of a believer to find the good in every circumstance, whether it be a happy or tough one.

Therefore, resilience is a crucial trait everyone must have to succeed. Islam offers a distinctive viewpoint on resilience; by adhering to its precepts and cultivating resilience, Muslims can face life's obstacles head-on with courage and assurance, knowing Allah (SWT) knows what is best for them.

Strategies for Cultivating Patience and Gratitude

Adopting a positive mindset (Husn al-Dhan) in adversity

Islam promotes positivism and an upbeat attitude toward life. Muslims are urged to put their trust in Allah's plan, even under trying circumstances, and to believe in His mercy and blessings. Muslims find solace and hope in believing in the efficacy of prayer and supplication.

An optimistic outlook can make all the difference in a world full of obstacles and uncertainties. Not only can positive thinking improve our mental and emotional health, but it also affects our behaviour, interpersonal connections, and general quality of life. The good news is that, with deliberate effort, cultivating a positive mindset is possible.

The Prophet Muhammad (PBUH) is a gift from Allah (SWT) to this Ummah, teaching us to face hardships and maintain our hope. By looking at the way he led his life, we can be inspired and encouraged to pursue perfection. The Prophet (PBUH) indeed faced greater trials than any other prophet before him. Despite enduring great hardships and being reduced to his knees by adversity, He (PBUH) placed his trust in Allah (SWT) and persisted in his progress.

We should adhere to the Prophet's (PBUH) Sunnah of optimistic thinking and sincerely focus on the positive aspects of things rather than their flaws. Since Allah (SWT) states in the Quran:

Allah knows, and you do not know. (Quran 2:216)

This is an extremely significant verse. Allah (SWT) is aware of the good that is there in difficulty, even if we are not. Perhaps persevering through that ordeal might be the key to reaching Jannah.

Keeping a positive mindset in the face of hardship helps you see the bright side, learn important lessons, and become stronger. Developing a positive outlook entails deliberately recognising the positive aspects of every circumstance, regardless of how bad it may appear.

This change in viewpoint enables you to face challenges with optimism and self-assurance in your capacity to conquer them. You can use the power of positive thinking to handle life's ups and downs with grace and fortitude by rephrasing obstacles as chances for learning and progress. Ultimately, having a positive view improves your well-being and makes your life more purposeful and meaningful.

Building faith in Allah's (SWT) wisdom can bring comfort and direction during difficult times. Accepting Allah's (SWT) limitless wisdom and realising that, even in the face of uncertainty, He knows what is best for you are essential to trusting Him. Knowing that every hardship is a step towards a bigger goal that Allah (SWT) has planned, this trust creates room for optimism.When facing difficulties, it is critical to remember that trials have a purpose. They challenge people to become stronger and wiser by acting as tests of faith and character. Accepting hardships in the context of one's trust in Allah's (SWT) divine purpose enables one to look beyond the current hardship and discover opportunities for spiritual and personal growth.

> *The Holy Prophet (PBUH) said that: "I am as my servant thinks of me. I am with him when he remembers me. If he mentions me within himself, I mention him within myself. If he mentions me in an assembly, I mention him in a better assembly. If he comes near to me a handspan, I come near to him the distance of a cubit. If he comes near to me the distance of a cubit, I come near to him the distance of two outspread arms. If he comes to me walking, I come to him running." (Sahih Muslim)*

In this crucial hadith, Allah (SWT) Himself tells us how important it is to think positively about Him. We must continue to think positively about our Creator and resist the devil's attempts to instil negative ideas in our heads. We shall profit more from Allah (SWT) in this life and the next if we think about Him in a pleasant light.

Positive thinking can improve our mental and emotional health, behaviour, interpersonal connections, and general quality of life. The good news is that cultivating a positive mindset is possible with deliberate effort. Let's discuss the benefits of positive thinking and see how to cultivate a more optimistic view of life.

Exercise gratitude: Cultivating patience and gratitude during adversity can significantly improve your overall well-being and help you navigate challenging times with a positive mindset. Being grateful is a great way to change our attention from what we lack to what we already have. Develop the everyday practice of expressing thankfulness. Every day, set aside some time to consider all the things, no matter how minor, for which you are thankful. By practising this, you can develop a more optimistic outlook by teaching your mind to recognise and value the good things in your life.

Adorn yourself with good things: Our mentality is greatly influenced by the individuals we spend time with and associate with. Seek out people who make you feel good and better. Take part in discussions that uplift and encourage you. Incorporate good influences into your surroundings, such as inspirational quotes, literature, and upbeat music. Positivity fosters a nurturing environment conducive to a positive growth mindset.

Prioritise solutions over problems: Instead of concentrating on problems, teach your mind to think about solutions. When presented with a problem, try not to get mired in negativity but instead focus on creating positive solutions. Developing a problem-solving mindset allows you to act and progress, promoting optimism.

Identify adverse thought patterns: Realising negative thoughts is the first step towards developing a positive mindset. Listen to your inner monologue and recognise self-limiting beliefs or recurrent negative thoughts. Once you identify these patterns, you can question and reframe the negative beliefs to replace them with more empowering and positive ones.

Put mindfulness into practice: Mindfulness is the practice of being completely present in the moment without passing judgement. Deep breathing and other mindfulness practices help calm the mind and bring it back to the present. By engaging in mindfulness practices, you can select constructive versus reactive responses by increasing your awareness of your thoughts and feelings.

Positivity is a lifetime process that calls for perseverance, self-awareness, and practice. Adopting an empowering and elevating perspective is the key to facing life's challenges head-on rather than trying to ignore them. Accept the power of positive thinking and see the amazing changes it brings about in your life.

Practising contentment (Qanaah) and trust in Allah (SWT)

It might be difficult to achieve contentment and feeling enough in a world where wants and desires seem to never end. However, a very spiritual Islamic habit known as "Qanaah" teaches us the value of being happy with what Allah (SWT) has provided us. Qanaah, commonly translated as "the feeling of enough," refers to contentment with what is not quite enough, letting go of the need for what is lacking, and making the most of what we have.

To be content is to accept Allah's (SWT) plan for us in peace. These guidelines assist us in achieving inner contentment and serenity by refocusing our attention from acquiring material possessions to strengthening our relationship with Allah (SWT).

Feeling good enough significantly affects many facets of human life. Surprisingly, it can provide us with true happiness and allow us to lead a happy, pure life based on thankfulness for Allah's (SWT) blessings.

This grateful mindset contributes to developing the concept of enough, generating a positive feedback loop that increases our sense of appreciation and contentment. When we learn to feel enough, we become more receptive to blessings because we become more appreciative and do not take things for granted.

To fully enjoy the sense of sufficiency, we need to shift our attention from wants to needs. Since it differs from person to person, the idea of enough is difficult to understand. What is sufficient for one person could not be sufficient for another. However, it is imperative that each of us set our standards for happiness.

> *The Prophet Muhammad (PBUH) emphasised being adequate as Muslims. He suggested: "If one of you sees a person who has excess wealth and a better appearance,*

then look at the person below him." (Sahih Bukhari and Sahih Muslim)

The idea of avoiding comparing one's possessions to others is strongly related to contentment. When we can put this mindset into practice and truly recognise how fortunate we are, we develop a deeper sense of gratitude and the idea that we are enough.

No matter how minor the pleasures and gifts may seem, if we honestly appreciate them, we will be genuinely grateful and constantly experience a sense of sufficiency. By doing this, we embrace a life of genuine fulfilment and learn about the richness and fullness of contentment.

Similarly, one of the greatest acts of worship is "Tawakkul", or dependence on Allah (SWT). It is a fundamental Islamic teaching. Our faith tells us that things will work out and that trials are chances for great blessings and rewards rather than penalties. Our duty as believers is to place our trust in Allah (SWT) in the hopes of receiving His blessings and pleasure. Having faith in Allah (SWT) is especially beneficial when one is afraid or uncertain.

The word "Wakala," which means to entrust something to someone, to place them in charge of something, and to rely on them for that, is the root of the word "Tawakkul." By giving your anxieties and fears to Allah (SWT) through Tawakkul, you strengthen your spiritual bond and recognise Him as the only one who can provide protection and direction.

This submissive behaviour gives you great emotional stability and bolsters your faith. When you become more resilient and able to handle life's obstacles with grace and fortitude, you relinquish control and put your faith in Allah (SWT). Accept Tawakkul, and watch how it changes your perspective and gives you a deep sense of serenity and faith in God's plan.

> *In the Quran, Allah says, "And He will provide him from [sources] he never could imagine. And whosoever puts his trust in Allah, and then He will suffice him. Verily, Allah will accomplish his purpose. Indeed Allah has set a measure for all things" (Quran 65:3)*

The Almighty Allah (SWT) makes it abundantly evident in the Holy Quran that Tawakkul is a must and not an option.

> *Allah says in the Quran in words: "...And put your trust in Allah if you are believers indeed" (Quran 5: 23)*

Tawakkul provides a form of illumination for our hearts and a way for us to pursue Allah (SWT) in a way that is unattainable through anything else. Two fundamental tenets support this aspect of the heart's nature: reliance on Allah (SWT) and faith in Allah (SWT).

> *Ibn Abbas reported: The Messenger of Allah, peace and blessings be upon him, would say, "O Allah, I have surrendered to you, and I have faith in you. I trust in you, and I have turned to you. I have contested my opponents for your sake. O Allah, I seek refuge in your power from going astray, for there is no God but you. You are the Living who never dies, while the jinn and humans die." (Sahih Bukhari)*

One can experience complete contentment and tranquillity by putting their trust in Allah (SWT). Muslims should never give up or grow dejected in trying times. Put all of your faith in Allah (SWT). Let us work to comprehend Tawakkul and incorporate it into our worldviews. We will observe that things will be addressed more quickly with His assistance, but Tawakkul will also free us from the daily agony and concerns brought on by the difficulties of this life. May Allah (SWT) support us through every challenging circumstance and grant us the fortitude to get through it.

Practising contentment (Qanaah) and trust (Tawakkul) in Allah (SWT) supports an optimistic mindset, which helps us stop worrying about what we do not have and instead focus on what we do have. This kind of thinking makes you happier and has a stronger spiritual life. Shukr and contentment lead to a more balanced and tranquil life by shifting our attention from worldly goals to higher spiritual fulfilment. They are strongly linked to general well-being.

Chapter Ten

Mindful Communication and Relationships

Mindful communication and healthy relationships are essential in Islam, emphasising respect, compassion, and understanding. Let's explore the principles of mindful communication within the context of Islamic teachings and provide practical steps for nurturing meaningful relationships.

Importance of Ethical Communication in Islam

Islam views ethical communication as a necessary talent that every Muslim ought to have. The significance of communication abilities is emphasised throughout the Quran and Hadith, which also offer advice on how to hone and enhance them.

> *Allah says in the Quran: "O you, who have believed, fear Allah and speak words of appropriate justice." (Quran 33:70)*

Islamic behaviour is centred on communication. Communication greatly impacts everyone's life since it serves as a source of information, fosters social interaction, changes people's attitudes, and much more. Effective communication is essential for conveying ideas and visions to others. It facilitates synchronisation and the transmission of instructions. It is impossible to express thoughts, ideas, and feelings without communication.

> *The Prophet Muhammad (PBUH) said: "Speak the truth even if it is bitter." (Ibn Majah)*

When you are on a mission or have a goal to accomplish, communication becomes even more important. You will be alone if you have no way to communicate. Effective communication is a highly valuable skill that is frequently disregarded and undervalued.

Communication is essential to disseminating ideas and messages. To accomplish the purpose, we must reach out to individuals, which makes communication essential to any accomplishment. Every individual has the innate ability to communicate; even the most inept person may communicate by doing.

> *Allah says in the Quran, "He has taught him to talk (and understand)" (Quran 55:4)*

In general, "the transfer of information" refers to a set of criteria by which the sender of a message can effectively communicate its message to the intended recipient. It could take several forms, such as nonverbal communication, including writing and gesturing, and vocal communication, which can occur in person and over the phone.

Even though there are many different ways to communicate, in-person contact is thought to be the most productive one, necessitating the greatest standards of etiquette and manners. Let's talk about some appropriate behaviours when interacting with others:

Upholding truthfulness (Sidq) and kindness (Rahmah) in speech

In Islam, there are no white lies! One of the lovely qualities of Allah's (SWT) commands is truthfulness. As-sidq (truthfulness) is a command from Allah (SWT); it is a necessary component of faith, a trait that all the prophets (PBUH) had to possess, and it is stated throughout the Quran!

> *The Messenger of Allah (PBUH) said, "Truthfulness (sidq) leads to righteousness (birr) and righteousness leads to the Garden. A person remains truthful until they are recorded as truthful in the sight of Allah. Lying leads to corruption (fisq), and corruption leads to the Fire. A person lies to the point that he is written down as an inveterate liar in the sight of Allah." (Sahih Bukhari)*

When communicating, the Sidq of the tongue indicates that the same thing should be said, in accordance with the actual circumstance. Falsehood is the act of speaking anything that is contrary to reality. Thus, Sadiq is the one who refrains from lying.

Upholding truthfulness (Sidq) and kindness (Rahmah) in speech is a core Islamic value.

> *The Quran emphasises, "O you who have believed, fear Allah and be with those who are truthful" (Quran 9:119)*

This highlights the importance of honesty in all interactions. Additionally, the Quran advises the necessity of kindness in communication:

"And speak to people good [words]" (Quran 2:83)

The Prophet (PBUH) also emphasised these values:

"He who believes in Allah and the Last Day must either speak good or remain silent." (Sahih Muslim)

This hadith reflects the importance of ensuring our words are beneficial and kind. By integrating truthfulness and kindness into our speech, we create an environment of trust and respect, reflecting Islam's moral and ethical teachings, which promote harmony and understanding among people.

Resolving conflicts with empathy and compassion (Mawaddah)

Any human connection will inevitably result in conflict, especially when different personalities, viewpoints, aspirations, and expectations exist. Conflict need not, however, be detrimental or destructive. In reality, if handled with empathy and compassion, disagreement can be a source of creativity, learning, and progress.

Compassion and empathy are the capacity to empathise with others, comprehend their emotions, and behave with kindness and consideration. Since they foster mutual respect, trust, and cooperation, they are crucial for nurturing effective relationships. Building a compassionate and empathetic culture can also help prevent or resolve problems.

Empathy acts as a link between people amid conflict despite their differences and conflicts. You may create an atmosphere where communication flourishes, conflicts ease, and agreements are made by genuinely understanding the feelings and viewpoints of others.

Islamic teachings emphasise mercy and understanding, and compassion is firmly anchored in empathy. To build relationships and promote harmony, imitate the Prophet's compassionate example and the emphasis on empathy in the Quran. Empathy and active listening foster comprehension, feelings, and goals in Islam.

Empathy, reducing the situation's intensity, and accepting different viewpoints are ways to peacefully resolve conflicts. Building trust and unity involves reflecting values, being present and demonstrating respect. Seek to discover common ground, build inclusive communities, and compassionately accept other points of view. Read Islamic Insights on Compassionate Communication to learn more about fostering empathy and compassionate communication.

It is recommended that you pay close attention to and gain a thorough understanding of the many viewpoints involved while resolving conflicts with empathy. You can handle conflicts with compassion and emotional intelligence by practising empathy in dispute resolution.

This strategy encourages respect for one another and peaceful solutions to difficult problems. Empathy can defuse conflicts and form paths to reconciliation. In addition to resolving current problems, giving empathy priority in conflict resolution procedures helps create the foundation for future harmonious and stronger relationships.

As you explore the pathways of Islamic viewpoints on empathy-based communication, picture yourself as a link between hearts. Allow Islam's teachings to help you comprehend and compassionately resolve disagreements.

Welcome variety with open arms and practise empathy in all of your interactions. Envision a world where empathy bridges are constructed, bringing souls together in harmony and comprehension. May you experience love, kindness, and the wonder of empathetically constructing bridges on your journey!

Building Meaningful Connections and Positive Relationships

In Islam, forming wholesome relationships is very important. For Allah (SWT), we are commanded by our faith to cultivate solid and wholesome relationships based on love, respect, and compassion for others. Our lives are significantly impacted by the intimate interactions we have with our loved ones. These relationships give us emotional support, company, and a feeling of belonging. They support, uplift, and inspire us as we face life's obstacles.

These familial ties, in turn, are highly valued in Islam. For the sake of Allah (SWT), our faith urges us to establish relationships based on love, respect, and compassion. These relationships foster our own personal development and well-being as well as the harmony and togetherness of our community. Therefore, maintaining good connections can positively impact not only ourselves but also the people around us and profoundly affect numerous facets of our lives.

Nurturing family ties (Silat al-Rahim)

A very important deed in the list of good actions is Silat ar-Rahim which involves preserving positive family dynamics through their creation, maintenance, or enhancement. "Silat" means "tie," and "rahim" means "womb," highlighting that relationships with family members are formed through the womb, or rahim.

Adam and Havaa, peace be upon them, were the first humans, and from them, the concept of family emerged. Islam places a high priority on maintaining family unity. Interestingly, the Arabic word for family, "usra", is derived from terms that mean unity, cohesion, and protection. For this reason, Muslims are often reminded to maintain links within their blood family through the verses of the Quran and the Seerah of our beloved Prophet (PBUH).

> *The Quran states: "O men, fear your Lord who created you from a single soul, and from it created its match, and spread many men and women from the two. Fear Allah in whose name you ask each other (for your rights), and fear (the violation of the rights of) the womb-relations. Surely, Allah is watchful over you." (Quran 4:1)*

The advantages and benefits of keeping familial relationships are substantial since Islam places a high value on them. In a similar vein, abandonment and cutting familial ties can have grave effects on an individual's life. Thus, it becomes essential that all Muslims receive a solid education about this crucial duty.

A typical, peaceful community must have its members communicating, interacting, and depending on one another. A person will engage with other people at all stages of their life. People one will often interact with more frequently are those in their family. Family relationships result in frequent interaction, so maintaining excellent relations with family members is essential. The following passage emphasises the significance of keeping harmonious relationships with every member of the family:

> *In another verse of the Quran, it is mentioned, "And worship Allah and do not assign partners with Him and be favourable unto parents and family members and the orphans and the destitute and the near neighbour and the distant neighbour and the traveller and your slaves. And Allah does not love one who is haughty and proud." (Quran 4:36)*

The issue is further highlighted by the large number of hadith that advise family kinship.

"Whoever believes in Allah and the Last Day, let him maintain the bonds of kinship." (Sahih Bukhari)

The Prophet (PBUH) said: "Learn your lineages to solidify your family ties. Indeed, keeping family ties causes love among the kinship, enriches the wealth, and increases the lifespan." (Tirmidhi)

Keeping your connections shows your faith. A genuine believer places the highest value on preserving positive relationships. The only reason to honour the deed is to appease Allah (SWT).

Keeping positive relationships with family members is very important and shows dedication to religion. Allah (SWT) values this action more than many others, such as prayer, fasting, and almsgiving. It counsels keeping strong relationships and taking the initiative to assist others in reestablishing contact. The believer who fortifies their family ties and brings about Allah's (SWT) blessings through well-being and nourishment will be rewarded.

Islamic Principles for Creating Strong Support Systems

As Muslims, we are obligated by our faith to establish solid communities based on the values of fraternity, solidarity, and unity. The Quran and the teachings of the Prophet Muhammad (PBUH) provide clear instructions on upholding brotherly relations, supporting one another in righteousness, and promoting the well-being of the community.

Fundamentally, brotherhood in Islam refers to the spiritual ties that bind believers. Muslims are regarded as spiritual brothers and sisters because they share the conviction that there is only one God.

> *The Quran states: "The believers are but brothers, so make settlement between your brothers" (Quran 49:10)*

This religious fraternity demands that people respect, work together, and lessen one another's burdens. It highlights how crucial it is to keep preconceived notions about one another at bay and foster harmony within the Muslim community.

> *"A Muslim is a brother of another Muslim, so he should not oppress him, nor should he hand him over to an oppressor. Whoever fulfilled the needs of his brother, Allah will fulfil his needs." (Sahih Muslim)*

Muslims are taught to be patient with one another, to be kind and understanding, and the teachings of the Prophet Muhammad (PBUH) advocate kindness, truth, guidance, and viewing other people's behaviour from the best perspective.

> *Prophet (PBUH) said, "Beware of suspicion, for suspicion is the most false of tales. Do not seek out faults, do not spy on each other, do not contend with each other, do not envy each other, do not hate each other, and do not turn away from each other. Rather, be servants of Allah as brothers" (Sahih Bukhari)*

In sum, Islam's concept of brotherhood fosters compassion and solidarity on several levels, ranging from familial relationships to religious fraternity. It does not support injustice, even as it encourages Muslims to treat one another with compassion and love. Islam prioritises compassion and justice for everyone, irrespective of background or religion. By preserving these values, Muslims can contribute to a more peaceful society and reinforce the ties that bind their community together.

Applying Prophetic etiquette (Adab) in interactions and social engagements

Good manners while communicating are among the factors that build positive social interactions. The golden rule states that you should treat people how you would like to be treated. Ethical behaviour is not limited to humans; it is necessary for all living things. Without it, one experiences constant decline, restlessness, anxiety, and a growing estrangement from the joy of their kind Creator.

The Messenger of Allah (PBUH) wants us to be constantly conscious of our behaviour and has given us a beautiful framework of moral and ethical behaviour. The Prophet (PBUH) offered himself to us as a perfect example to follow in this sense.

> *Allah (SWT) says in the Quran: "There has certainly been for you in the Messenger of Allah an excellent pattern." (Quran 33:21)*

The Messenger of Allah (PBUH) teaches us several important lessons:

- Ensure our conversations are beneficial so the person we speak with can learn something productive and useful.
- Use simple, polite, and easy language to connect easily with others, conveying love, mutual respect, and sincerity.
- Avoid making things hard or complicated, leading to anger,

hatred, and division.

- Stay silent when angry to control emotions effectively. Being quiet immediately helps maintain self-control over anger and emotions.

These principles ensure our interactions are positive, respectful, and conducive to learning and harmony.

Thus, mindful communication and fostering healthy relationships are central to Islamic teachings. Upholding truthfulness and kindness in speech, resolving conflicts with empathy, nurturing family ties, and creating strong support systems are crucial to ethical behaviour. By applying these principles, we ensure our interactions are positive, respectful, and conducive to learning and harmony, thus reflecting the moral and ethical teachings of Islam.

Chapter Eleven

Evening Reflection and Gratitude Practice

Humans are endowed with the capacity for thought and reasoning by Allah (SWT). Compared to all other creatures, humans possess free will due to this characteristic that sets them apart from animals.

We can live and prosper in this world because of the benefit that Allah (SWT) has bestowed upon us; without it, we would not be able to advance in this life or find salvation hereafter. Thus, we can see that thinking, reasoning, and reflecting are the fundamental steps that lead to Allah (SWT), who constantly tells us to do so in the Quran.

> *Surely in the creation of the heavens and the earth, and the alternation of the night and day are signs for people of understanding, those who remember Allah while standing, sitting or reclining, and reflect in the creation of the heavens and the earth, (saying): "Our Lord! You have not created this in vain. Glory to you! Save us, then, from the chastisement of the Fire!"(Quran 3:190-191)*

All of this is reflection when you consider the cosmos from an astronomical, biological, or chemical perspective. All of this is a component of the 'Ibadah and 'Ilm that will create ulama who fear Allah (SWT). You will gain enlightenment in the Islamic sense and become closer to Allah (SWT) if you sequester yourself and consider the wisdom of creation behind the material you study. Let's explore how to incorporate a reflection routine in our life.

Implementing Evening Adhkar (Supplications)

Adhkar is a set of invocations prescribed by our beloved Prophet (PBUH) to be uttered for the remembrance of Allah (SWT). As a result, the Prophet's (PBUH) Sunnah includes the recital of Adhkar.

> *It is reported that: "The Prophet (PBUH) was asked, 'Which deed is more virtuous?' "He (PBUH) answered, 'To depart with one's tongue preoccupied with the remembrance of Allah (PBUH).'" (Musnad Ahmad)*

Dhikr awakens our hearts to our creator's love and light and ensures we are united to Him. It is the act of remembering Allah (SWT) by giving thanks, honouring, and praising him. It can also refer to different dua forms. Praise of Allah (SWT) strengthens our Tawhid (conviction that Allah is one). We become aware of Allah's Might and Magnificence.

Morning and evening duas are more beneficial than other times of the day when one remembers Allah (SWT). We shall now discuss the advantages of evening Adhkar as well as appropriate behaviour.

Evening Adhkar provides spiritual peace and protection and strengthens faith. It fosters forgiveness and blessings while reducing stress and promoting emotional stability. Reciting Adhkar prepares one spiritually for the night, offering a sense of security. To practise appropriately, focus on the recitations with sincerity and respect, maintain consistency, and choose a quiet place. Ensure mindfulness of the meanings and perform the Adhkar with gratitude and humility. Following these behaviours aligns with the Sunnah of the Prophet (PBUH), enriching your spiritual and emotional well-being.

Evening Supplications

- **Ayat ul-Kursi**

Upon reaching evening, the person who recites it will be safe from the Jinn (evil) till morning. Nothing but death will stand between the people who recite Aayat ul-Kursi after performing each required Salah, bringing them closer to paradise.

> *Allah! None has the right to be worshiped but He, the Ever living, the One Who sustains and protects all that exists. Neither slumber nor sleep overtakes Him. To Him belongs whatever is in the heavens and whatever is on earth. Who is he that can intercede with Him except with His Permission? He knows what happens to them (His creatures) in this world and what will happen to them in the Hereafter. And they will never compass anything of His Knowledge except that which He wills. His Kursi extends over the heavens and the earth, and He feels no fatigue in guarding and preserving them. And He is the Most High, the Most Great. (Quran: 2:255)*

- **The Tahleel**

Ten times during the evening, recite this. Reciting the aforementioned supplication 100 times throughout the night is another Sunnah practice. The Prophet Muhammad (PBUH) emphasised that reciting Tahleel can lead to the forgiveness of sins. He said, "The best of supplications is that of the Day of 'Arafah, and the best of what I and the Prophets before me have said is:

> *"None has the right to be worshipped but Allah alone, who has no partner. His is the dominion and His is the praise and He is Able to do all things." (Sahih Bukhari)*

- **Sayyid ul-Istighfaar**

Once in the evening, recite. A person will belong to the people of Paradise if they recite it throughout the day with great faith and pass away that same day before dusk. The same is true for those who read it at night.

> *"O Allah, You are my Lord; there is none worthy of worship but you. You created me, and I am your slave. I am upon your covenant and your promise to the best of my ability. I seek Your Protection from the evil that I have done. I acknowledge your blessings upon me, and I acknowledge my sins. So forgive me, for no one forgives sins but you." (Sahih Bukhari)*

- **For daily protection**

Recite three times in the evening. If someone says this in the morning, they will not experience sudden affliction until the evening, and whoever repeats it in the morning will not experience sudden affliction until the morning.

> *"In the Name of Allah, Who with His Name nothing can cause harm neither in the earth nor in the heavens, and He is the All-Hearing, the All-Knowing." (Abu Daud)*

- **Praising Allah (SWT)**

Read aloud 100 times at night. Saying it 100 times atones for your sins, even if they are as great as the ocean's foam. On the Day of Judgement, nobody will bring anything superior to it save the one who has increased or done the same as him.

> *"Glory be to Allah and all Praise belongs to Allah."*
> *(Sahih Muslim)*

These few evening supplications are a powerful practice that offers numerous spiritual and practical benefits to those who observe them regularly. In sum, evening supplications offer comprehensive benefits: they protect from harm, secure forgiveness, promote spiritual growth and bring one closer to Allah (SWT). Integrating these practices into one's daily routine enhances faith, fortifies the spirit, and ensures divine protection and blessings.

Seeking forgiveness (Tawbah) and Repenting

We are all sinners. We commit sins without even realising their effects on us. Not only does Allah (SWT) know about our sins, but we also do. They have an immediate effect on our neighbourhoods, families, and eventually the Ummah as a whole.

Sins drive us from Allah (SWT) and bring about His wrath and punishment. Sins take away barakah and make the body and heart weaker. Sins keep us from performing good deeds, hinder the acceptance of our sacrifices, bring about a terrible death, and cause misery in the afterlife.

However, the believer feels regret and repentance as soon as he realises that he has disobeyed Allah (SWT) and committed a sin. The humble believer comes to his Lord in full humility, regretful and ashamed, relying on Allah's mercy, asking for His pardon.

He swears he will not carry out the same deed twice. This act is called "Tawbah and Istighfaar" in Shariah. The believer is elevated and becomes closer to Allah (SWT) as a result of his deep sense of sorrow and remorse for committing a sin, his vow to never do it again, and his complete faith in Allah's promised mercy and forgiveness.

> *The Messenger of Allah (PBUH) said, "Indeed, when the servant commits a sin, a black dot appears on his heart. When he desists, seeks forgiveness and repents, his heart is polished clean. But if he commits a sin again, it increases until it covers his heart. (Tirmidhi)*

> *And that is the 'ran' (rust) which Allah mentioned: "No indeed! Rather what they have been doing has rusted their hearts" (Quran 83:14)*

The mark of a believer is sincere Tawbah or repentance; this involves sincerely turning to Allah with all of one's heart and humbly offering an apology.

> *Allah (SWT) says, "O believers! Turn to Allah in sincere repentance, so your Lord may erase your sins and admit you into Gardens, under which rivers flow..." (Quran 66:8)*

We should take stock of all our transgressions throughout our lives and feel deeply sorry for them. We should reflect on how little we have praised Allah's (SWT) kindness and generosity towards us and how we often misuse these same benefits to disobey Him. We should consider how, in spite of the multitude of our crimes, Allah al-Sittir

(The Concealer of Crimes) does not reveal himself to us. This should fill us with great regret and guilt.

However, a committed tawbah can turn a sinner's path to Paradise. A person may sin but then genuinely turn to tawbah. When tawbah is heartfelt, it involves constant reflection on the sin, fear of it, deep regret, sorrow, and a sense of embarrassment before Allah (SWT). With a humbled heart, the individual bows his head in humility before Allah (SWT) and prays and begs Him in dua, striving to make up for the transgression by performing other good deeds, to the point where Shaytan himself expresses regret for having led the person to stray. As a result, the sinner's admission into Paradise can be attributed to this sincere repentence.

Allah (SWT) grants tawbah as a gift. We can only make tawbah when Allah (SWT) permits us to. When we turn to Allah (SWT) in repentance, He receives it from us first and then responds to us.

To avoid future regrets, we should make tawbah right now. There is a belief that if the dead could speak to us from their grave, they would express their deepest wish to be allowed to return to this life—even for a brief while—to make sincere tawbah to Allah (SWT).

Cultivating a State of Spiritual Tranquillity (Sukoon)

The pursuit of inner tranquillity is one of our deepest aspirations as humans. Our primary motivation is their desire for peace and the fact that no matter what we do, we always want to live in harmony and tranquillity.

The path to tranquillity is not a condition of being, just like anything else in Islam. To arrive at the point when we are at peace with ourselves, there is a path that must be travelled and actions that must be taken. There is a part of us that has always wanted to be at peace. We all have a hole inside of us that only Allah (SWT) can fill. Imam Ibn al-Qayyim discusses this in great detail;

> *"In the heart, there is a sense of untidiness which can only be gathered by turning to Allah. In the heart there is a sense of loneliness which can only be removed by coming closer to Allah. And in the heart, there is fear and anxiety, which only leaves by fleeing to Allah. And in the heart, there is a sense of regret, which can only be removed by being satisfied with Allah." (Imam Ibn al-Qayyim)*

When used in reference to the Quran, the term "sukoon" describes a peaceful, serene, and tranquil state that permeates its verses. It stands for the inner peace and contentment that people might have when they follow the teachings and guidance of the Quran. Sukoon, which arises from a connection with the sacred book and its message, can be a state of contentment, peace of mind, and spiritual fulfilment.

The crucial query is: How may one attain the inner tranquillity and peace of mind that all people aspire to? This question is addressed in the passages of Allah Almighty's (SWT) last revelation.

> *Allah says in the Quran: "Those who believe, their hearts find peace and tranquillity in the remembrance of Allah; it is only in the remembrance of Allah that the heart will find contentment." (Quran 13:28)*

Thus, the best way to establish lasting tranquillity and peace of mind is to spend your time remembering Allah (SWT). That is the direct path to achieving calm and peace of mind, but do not think that in today's society, that is an easy feat.

In the modern world, we face many challenges, including numerous distractions and unhelpful expectations. Let's examine a few practical strategies that can support you in consistently achieving inner peace and tranquillity.

Winding down with mindful practices before bedtime

Establishing a calm and restful bedtime routine is essential for achieving spiritual tranquillity and mental peace. Incorporating mindful practices into your pre-sleep ritual can significantly enhance your overall sense of well-being.

Dedicating time to mindfulness and spiritual reflection before bed fosters a more peaceful, rejuvenating sleep, thereby nurturing your inner tranquillity.

Mindfulness meditation is a useful technique for applying mindfulness to sleep aids. This approach involves paying attention to your thoughts and sensations while primarily focusing on your breathing. Try not to ponder about the future or your prior experiences while doing this.

The goal of mindfulness meditation is to induce a state of relaxation and divert your attention from your everyday problems.

Two steps to practising mindfulness meditation:

Calm concentration: Select a peaceful method of concentration. You can maintain your composure by inhaling deeply. You can repeatedly inhale and exhale while performing these relaxing techniques.

Unwind: After concentrating on how you are feeling, let go and stop worrying about how you are doing. Take a deep breath and bring your calm concentration back to whatever you selected when you feel your thoughts straying.

You must be in a peaceful frame of mind when using mindfulness practices to help you fall asleep. The following elements could support your ability to stay composed and focused:

You will need to be in a calm spot to relax. This does not imply that silence is required in the surroundings. Steer clear of noisy environments because where you are matters when attempting to unwind. Pick a position you feel most comfortable. Before starting your mindfulness meditation, consider lying in bed.

To effectively engage in mindfulness meditation, you must focus on the here and now and ignore what is happening outside of yourself. To keep your mind from straying, keep your breathing rhythm or concentrate on a mental image.

Here are some Islamic mindful practices you might find helpful before bedtime:

Engage in Dhikr: recite "SubhanAllah," "Alhamdulillah," and "Allahu Akbar." You can also recite the Tasbih of Fatimah: "SubhanAllah" 33 times, "Alhamdulillah" 33 times, and "Allahu Akbar" 34 times.

Reading the Last Two Verses of Surah Al-Baqarah: The Prophet (PBUH) recommended reciting these verses before sleeping, as they offer protection and blessings.

Reflect on the Day: Spend a few moments reflecting on your day, seeking forgiveness for any shortcomings and giving thanks for the blessings.

Perform Wudu (Ablution): If possible, perform wudu before sleeping. It is a way of purifying yourself and is considered a Sunnah of the Prophet (PBUH).

Dua (Supplication): Make Dua for protection, guidance, and forgiveness.

Incorporating these practices into your bedtime routine can help create a sense of tranquillity and connection with Allah (SWT) before you sleep.

Expressing gratitude (Shukr) for blessings and experiences of the day

Expressing gratitude, or Shukr, for the day's blessings can profoundly impact your well-being and spiritual connection. Because of the numerous favours and bounties that Allah, may He be adored and exalted, has showered upon His slaves in both the spiritual and material realms, He is the one who is most deserving of people's gratitude and appreciation. We are obligated by Allah to acknowledge and praise Him for His bounties.

Expressing gratitude to Allah (SWT) for His favours looks like this:

- Accepting in your heart that Allah is the one who bestows these gifts;

- Acknowledging with your tongue the gifts you have received from Him;

- Preventing your physical senses from seeing or hearing any wrongdoing or evil, and expressing gratitude with your physical senses.

Start your morning with a moment of reflection, appreciating the gift of a new day. Throughout the day, take mindful pauses to acknowledge small blessings, like a kind gesture or the beauty of nature, and verbally or mentally express thanks whenever something positive happens.

In the evening, reflect on the day's events and write three to five things you are thankful for in a gratitude journal. Offer prayers of thanks, acknowledging both joys and challenges as opportunities for growth. Share your blessings by helping others and expressing gratitude to loved ones through simple "thank you" or notes of appreciation. End your day with a peaceful heart, content with the experiences it brought, knowing that each day contributes to your growth and well-being.

To show your gratitude to your Lord for all the blessings He has bestowed upon you, you must first acknowledge in your heart that Allah (SWT), may He be exalted, is the Giver of these favours and the Bestower. You then venerate Him, attribute it to Him, and acknowledge that with your tongue. You thank Him for giving you new life when you wake up from sleep, providing you with food and drink, bestowing blessings upon you, and so on with every blessing you see in your life.

Incorporating reflection, supplications, and gratitude into our evening routines fosters spiritual tranquillity and strengthens our connection with Allah (SWT). Let's sincerely embrace these rituals, allowing them to transform our hearts and draw us closer to Allah (SWT).

Chapter Twelve

Conclusion

As we conclude this journey into the realm of mindfulness in Islam, it is important to reflect on the profound lessons and practices we have explored together. The essence of mindfulness, or Taqwa, is deeply embedded in Islamic teachings, and embracing these principles can lead to a balanced life filled with joy and gratitude.

Mindfulness in Islam is not merely a contemporary concept but a timeless practice that has been emphasised by our Prophet Muhammad (PBUH) and found in the teachings of the Quran. It involves being fully present in our actions, thoughts, and interactions and maintaining a constant awareness of Allah (SWT). This spiritual awareness is the cornerstone of a mindful Muslim's life, guiding every action and decision.

Starting with our morning rituals, we see the significance of beginning our day with the Fajr prayer, which sets a foundation of mindfulness. This prayer, offered at dawn, not only awakens our spiritual consciousness but also establishes a routine of gratitude and reflection. By acknowledging Allah's blessings from the start of our day, we set a positive and mindful tone for the hours ahead.

Daily Quranic reflections further deepen our mindfulness practice. Recitation and contemplation of the Quran (Tadabbur) connect us to divine wisdom and guidance. By integrating Quranic teachings into our daily lives, we align our actions with our spiritual values, fostering a sense of purpose and direction.

Dhikr, the remembrance of Allah (SWT), is crucial in cultivating mindfulness. Engaging in regular dhikr helps us connect with Allah (SWT) throughout the day, keeping our hearts and minds focused on His presence. This practice not only brings peace and tranquillity but reinforces our spiritual resilience.

Mindful eating and nutrition, guided by the principles of Halal and Tayyib, remind us to approach food with gratitude and moderation. By being conscious of what we consume, we honour our bodies as gifts from Allah (SWT) and practice self-discipline, a vital aspect of mindfulness.

Self-care and well-being, rooted in prophetic guidance, underscore the importance of maintaining physical, mental, and emotional health. Islam encourages us to care for ourselves, recognising that a healthy body and mind are essential for fulfilling our spiritual obligations. Prioritising self-care allows us to serve Allah (SWT) and our communities more effectively.

Mindfulness in prayer, particularly in Salah, enhances our concentration (Khushu) and deepens our connection with Allah (SWT). Understanding the spiritual dimensions of Salah transforms it from a mere ritual to a profound experience of worship. Being fully present in our prayers elevates our spiritual practice and draws us closer to Allah (SWT).

Practising patience (Sabr) and gratitude (Shukr) are fundamental virtues in Islam that contribute to a mindful life. These qualities enable us to navigate life's challenges with resilience and grace. By cultivating patience and gratitude, we develop a positive outlook and strengthen our faith.

Mindful communication and relationships highlight the importance of ethical interactions and meaningful connections. Islam teaches us to engage with others respectfully and compassionately, fostering positive relationships that contribute to our overall well-being. By practising mindful communication, we build a supportive and loving community.

Evening reflection and gratitude practices help us end our day with mindfulness. Implementing evening Adhkar (supplications) and reflecting on the day's events cultivate a state of spiritual tranquillity (Sukoon). This practice allows us to acknowledge Allah's (SWT) blessings, seek His forgiveness, and prepare for a restful night.

In conclusion, embracing mindfulness in Islam is a transformative journey that enriches our spiritual, mental, and physical well-being. By incorporating these daily habits into our lives, we nurture our souls and create a balanced life filled with joy and gratitude. Let's strive to be mindful Muslims, constantly aware of Allah's (SWT) presence and guided by His divine wisdom in all aspects of our lives.

Find Out More

Website: www.barakahinbusiness.com

Socials: @barakahinbusiness

If you enjoyed this book, kindly leave a review to help expand our reach so others may benefit also.

www.ingramcontent.com/pod-product-compliance
Lightning Source LLC
Chambersburg PA
CBHW072058110526
44590CB00018B/3221